The Internal Auditor's
Information Security Handbook

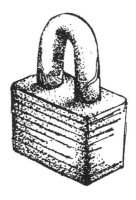

The Internal Auditor's
INFORMATION SECURITY HANDBOOK

Barry J. Wilkins

The Institute of Internal Auditors, Inc.

ISBN 0-89413-080-3

Library of Congress Catalog Card Number 79-91362

78210-Dec79

Foreword

Many reasons make this handbook a necessary part of internal auditing and management libraries.
- It is the first auditor's handbook devoted solely to the subject of information security.
- It gives a comprehensive treatment of the subject.
- A "how-to" book, it contains 20 checklists which organizations can use to develop information-security programs of their own.
- It provides an information-security audit guide and evaluation table for conducting audits.
- It offers constructive ideas and practical solutions to a multitude of information-security problems.
- It discusses data-processing security in layman's terms.
- The controls recommended ensure privacy and provide timely solutions which comply with the requirements of pending legislation.
- It discusses methods of obtaining executive management visibility.
- It presents innovative approaches to information-security programs that do not negatively impact the needs of the organization; at the same time, it maximizes the benefits of the information-security resources.
- It analyzes new audit techniques so information-security audit efforts can be concentrated on the important areas.
- It recommends audit tests and penetration attempts in certain situations.

Barry Wilkins

About the Author

Barry Wilkins is the corporate internal audit data processing manager for IBM Corporation. He has been in internal auditing for more than six years and has conducted many information-security audits. Consequently, his opinions are based on extensive practical experience.

Wilkins received a master's degree in financial management from Pace University. His thesis on information security, in fulfillment of the degree requirements, serves as the basis of this handbook.

A guest speaker at many professional association meetings and seminars, including The Institute of Internal Auditors, Inc., and the EDP Auditors' Association, he also participated in an invitational task force on Audit and Evaluation of Computer Security, sponsored by the National Bureau of Standards. With Bill Murray, he coauthored Section VII, "Auditing Administrative and Physical Security in a Computer Environment," of the resulting U.S. government publication (No. 500-19).

The thoughts, ideas, opinions, and discussions presented in this handbook are the author's and do not necessarily reflect the thinking of the author's past or present employers or any professional associations or any other individual.

Acknowledgments

To convert a master's thesis into a useful handbook requires the efforts of many people, and this handbook is no exception. I would like to express gratitude to the following friends and associates, as well as to my family, who helped in its preparation:

William Perry and Fred Palmer for their ideas, sponsorship, encouragement, and patience.

John Bowman, Nick Campbell, Bob Courtney, Russ Crawford, Cliff Jones, Richard McLaughlin, Dick Morron, Bill Murray, Conrad Naef, Joe Rogers, Joe Rosetti, Huck Wood, and Mike Zeoli, who provided me with invaluable ideas and candid comments.

My thesis advisor, Dean Weiss of Pace University, whose patience and wisdom enabled the successful completion of the work.

Vangie Kenneally, who devoted her time to typing the initial thesis manuscript.

My family for understanding and accepting my absences at family get-togethers.

My wife, Barbara, who has been, as always, the mainstay of my strength and morale. She also typed the manuscript, was my favorite critic, and put up with the inconvenience, disturbance, and neglect which the writing of a thesis and a handbook and the pursuance of a master's degree inevitably entail.

The responsibility for errors or omissions — is mine. The information presented herein represents or supports my own opinions.

B.W.

Introduction

The security crisis taking place in industry today is not limited to the theft of consumer goods or embezzlement. In fact, the future of many companies may depend on their ability to protect their proprietary information.

The concern for information security has come about as a result of the need to create, transmit, and process more and more proprietary information faster and more efficiently than ever before. In recent years, management has been preoccupied with the pressing need to implement new and better methods and equipment' for processing information to meet the needs of business. But information security technology has not kept pace with information processing technology, and industrial espionage is no longer in the realm of "science fiction"; it is real.

The intellectual assets of any organization are the intelligence and ideas within the organization; these are the intangibles that the future of any organization depends on. Almost all organizations are engaged in gathering intelligence about the competition. They have professional staffs (called "marketing research" or "competitive analysis") whose job is to keep abreast of the marketplace and the strengths and weaknesses of the competition. In the governmental arena, agencies like the Central Intelligence Agency (CIA) are responsible for gathering information about threats to our national security.

The majority of this intelligence gathering is done in a legal, overt manner; however, the number of individuals and organizations engaged in covert intelligence-gathering activities is growing. Today, there are many documented instances of information-security breaches. Surprisingly, many court cases have alleged the theft of trade secrets where both the plaintiff and the defendant were large, well-known organizations. This is not to say that technology vendors are not providing security controls; on the contrary, they are building them into their products. Numerous examples can be cited where technological improvements have provided better security. However, security controls and management controls have been generally underutilized.

The internal auditing profession has not been as active in reviewing information security as in reviewing financial controls and the protection afforded other physical assets. It is time to accept the challenge and assist management in ensuring that the organization's proprietary information is protected against both overt and covert attempts at unauthorized access.

This handbook provides a comprehensive information-security program, checklists, and an audit approach to assessing the effectiveness of the information-security program within an organization. Its scope is limited to information security, the prevention of information from being disclosed to an unauthorized recipient.

CONTENTS

CHECKLISTS

FIGURES

1

The Information-Security Issue

Today's business environment requires the generation and distribution of more proprietary information than ever before. As companies continue to grow, diversify, and geographically disperse, proprietary information is no longer maintained by only a few key executives. Instead, the number of employees with authorized need to know increases, and the need for generating more proprietary information increases correspondingly. Also, rapidly changing technologies necessitating large expenditures in research and development and keen competition requiring innovative marketing strategies contribute to the increasing generation of proprietary information.

The development of new methods and media to create and transmit information further complicates the problem of preventing proprietary information from falling into the hands of unauthorized recipients. Because these sophisticated computer systems can automate more proprietary information than ever before, new security controls and procedures are needed. Some organizations are centralizng computer operations while decentralizing access. They are storing all of the organization's records in one computer center and making access to these records available through terminals in offices around the world. Multiple access to these consolidated data banks has increased exposure to loss of proprietary information.

The use of time-sharing systems and the ability to transmit bulk data files from one computer center to another electronically further make organizations vulnerable to security leaks. The move by many organizations to distributed data processing, where proprietary information is duplicated at multiple locations, also creates a set of information-security concerns for management and the internal auditor. The subjects of data processing auditing and security in a data processing environment are receiving a great deal of emphasis, and excellent reference material on these subjects is available. The Institute of Internal Auditors, Inc., has released a definitive statement on data processing auditing techniques.[1]

---

[1] *Systems Auditability and Control*, 3 vols. (Altamonte Springs, FL: The Institute of Internal Auditors, Inc., 1977).

More Than Data Processing Security

Some words of caution are necessary here. Information security is not limited to data processing. Although the subjects of data processing auditing and security appear frequently in the news media and many internal audit staffs are occupied in establishing qualified data processing audit functions, the subject of information security encompasses more than data processing security. In fact, appropriating information from a computer center may not be any more difficult than obtaining the information from an employee's desk. It can be assumed the perpetrator will select the easiest method to accomplish the objective. The protection of information in a data processing environment is an integral part of an overall information security program, but data processing is only one of many areas in an organization where information can be exposed to unauthorized access. Information is *created* in the data processing environment, but it is *distributed* and *used outside* that environment.

Also, the new methods for creating and transmitting proprietary data are not limited to computer technology. Advances in reproduction have made possible the teleprocessing of documents over phone lines, and modern typewriters have the capability to record information on magnetic cards or tapes. Both are examples of how new media which facilitate creating and transmitting proprietary information can create additional information security exposures. They point up the fact that concentration of audit and operating management attention on data processing security alone will result in significant information security exposures.

Important Business Information Vulnerable

It is not the intent of this handbook to prove the need for information security; a review of the news media will do that. Briefly, however, it should be noted that internal auditors must focus their attention on the importance of the information-security problem. Four major reasons make the problem critical.

The rewards that can be obtained from misappropriating information are often much higher than the rewards involved in stealing cash, precious metals, or other physical assets. New product design specifications can bring substantial rewards from a company's competitor. They can save the competitor millions of dollars in design expense and shorten the lead time to enter the market. New weapons designs can bring tremendous rewards from foreign governments.

While the rewards are higher, the risks of being caught and prosecuted for stealing information are lower. Information can be stolen without physically removing it and often without leaving any indication of the theft. A document can be memorized, copied, or secretly filmed. As compared to other types of theft, theft of information can be instantaneous, requiring only a simple act

2

executed in a matter of seconds. There is not even need to conceal the act through years of bookkeeping entries. Because the subject of information security is relatively new, the controls necessary to prevent and detect information loss are not widely implemented; they change, too, as information processing technology changes. This may be the major reason that the risks associated with the misappropriation of information, as compared to other assets, are minimized.

The loss of proprietary information to the organization can have more severe consequences than a million-dollar payroll fraud. Unauthorized access to new product design specifications, marketing strategies, customer satisfaction surveys, or customers' master lists may give the competition an advantage that will severely jeopardize a company or even bankrupt it. Unauthorized access to proprietary government information could threaten national defense.

Information security is not a traditional area of internal audit involvement. Therefore, many organizations have not yet realized the benefits from internal auditing emphasis on information security.

Anyone not convinced of the need for information security should read the news media and ask operating and security managers in his or her organization or peers in other organizations if they have experienced any information security incidents. The results will be surprising. Today there are numerous documented incidents of information misappropriation, most of which have been detected inadvertently. Also, questions to peers in other organizations and managers within one's own organization will probably result in known examples of information security incidents being explained.

Information security is an important and complex problem in industry today and must be addressed by internal auditors and management. As Jan R. Reber, a well-known author on the subject, states:

> It is crucial to every corporation that it fully realize itself to be the object of someone's intelligence process every day it continues to exist as a corporate entity.[2]

Visibility and Management Awareness

While the need for information security is becoming more visible, the subject has not yet commanded the attention it requires. Many organizations have not yet become aware of the significance of the problem, because information security is a relatively new phenomenon. While many books and articles are being written about it, it may be years before management understands the importance of information security and gives it the proper attention.

---

[2] Jan E. Reber, "The Essence of Industrial Espionage," *Asset Protection Journal*, 1 (Spring 1975): 7.

The Practising Law Institute, in its 1977 publication *Protecting and Profiting from Trade Secrets,*[3] states that, in the United States, fewer than half of the states (approximately 20) have trade secret statutes. This fact verifies that concern for information security is not as great as it should be.

There is a critical need for better publicizing information security leaks in business and government. The American Management Association now estimates the cost of crimes against business to be between $40-$50 billion. This is an increase of 20 to 30% from their 1975 estimate. While available information does not effectively summarize information security losses, they appear to be very substantial.[4]

Until there is better reporting and until new laws are created, internal auditors should ensure there is a sufficient level of awareness and concern in their organizations.

Internal Auditor's Role

The internal auditing profession must accept the challenge, face up to its responsibilities, and assist management in implementing effective information-security programs. The complexity of the internal auditor's role will vary with the organization. In those organizations where management has emphasized information security and written requirement statements, the auditor's role will be to test for compliance. However, in organizations where management has not recognized the importance of information security, the auditor's role will be more difficult. It will be up to the auditor to demonstrate through audits not only the *lack* of information-security controls but also the *need* for these controls. Because information security has both dollar and labor costs, this may not be an easy task.

Implementation of an information security program can have a negative impact on profits and productivity. In today's environment where expense control and productivity are major management issues, the internal auditor will have to demonstrate tangibly the need for information security; it may not be enough to present the need on a philosophical basis. Tangibly demonstrating this need to executive management may be the greatest challenge the internal auditor will encounter. The internal auditor may have to obtain documented incidents; determine the policies and practices of other, similar organizations; or bring a summary of incidents that occurred within the organization to management's attention. Staging an incident, without involving audit privilege, where unauthorized access is gained to highly proprietary information can be another

---

[3] Practising Law Institute, *Protecting and Profiting from Trade Secrets,* Course Handbook Series, No. 8 (New York: Practising Law Institute, 1977), p. 10.

[4] American Management Association, *Crimes Against Business* (New York: American Management Association, 1977), p. 7.

effective way to demonstrate need. Internal audit penetrations of this kind are discussed in Chapter 6.

The internal auditor should also demonstrate that an effective information-security program can be implemented at a reasonable cost and without significant impact on other needs of the organization. Implementation of an overall security and control program (including information security) can have a positive impact on profit and productivity by reducing errors and eliminating unnecessary corrective effort.

The basic requirements and resultant expense of such a program will vary. A government organization concerned with national defense may require extensive information security at great expense, whereas like measures in a business enterprise may be neither practical nor economical. Accordingly, internal auditors must be sure that their information-security recommendations are both practical and reasonable·for the organization being reviewed. They must strive to reach the right balance between information security on the one hand and the objectives of the organization on the other.

As with any internal auditing program, the keys to the effectiveness of an information-security audit are the approach and checklist developed as a guideline. Chapter 6 discusses an audit approach for information security, and checklists are provided at the end of the applicable section. These should provide a good base on which an organization can build its information-security audit program tailored to its own unique environment.

Management's Role

Management must take a top-down approach. Information security requires additional controls that can impact the performance of other duties employees may be evaluated on. It is necessary, therefore, for executive management to clarify to employees the importance of the area and to advise employees that they will be measured on their implementation of the program. The probability of having an effective information security program without direct executive management involvement is minimal. This is why the internal auditor's first task should be to obtain executive management's support.

Executive management must realize that an effective information security program costs money, and it must be willing to pay the price. Information security is more complex and encompassing than plant security and requires more than the traditional security measures and responsibilities of the guard force. Locks, keys, and after-hour patrols are not sufficient.

Norman Jaspan outlines some of the management rationalizations that are no longer tolerable in today's business environment.

"Our auditors check our controls, and our protection department double checks our employees . . . We are aware of everything that is going on. It can't happen here . . ." "I trust him implicitly." . . . "They're going to steal from you anyway; there's nothing you can do about it." . . . "We have set up a reserve." . . . "I'm insured."[5]

Not only is management responsible for protecting its information, but also it is morally liable for creating a work environment free of temptations. Otherwise, even honest employees might go bad.

Management has the ultimate responsibility for information security. The owner or creator of information is the most knowledgeable concerning its value to the organization. It is his or her responsibility to ensure its proper protection. Management must ensure also that information service groups such as the computer room or secretarial pool protect information. An effective information security program requires the efforts of each and every employee; however, it is line management's responsibility to ensure a high level of employee awareness.

Applicability

Any organization having information which, if disclosed to an unauthorized recipient, would seriously affect the organization's objectives can apply the principles contained in this handbook. Following is a partial list of types of information which, if publicized or taken out of context, could cause the organization embarrassment.

Current Product
Customer-satisfaction surveys
Customer's master list
Customer's list with products installed
Marketing surveys
Planned enhancements
List of distributors
Design specifications
Cost figures

New Product
Design specifications
Marketing surveys
Competitive analysis reports
Potential customer list

---

[5] Norman Jaspan, *Mind Your Own Business* (Englewood Cliffs, New Jersey: Prentice-Hall, Inc., 1974), pp. 16-80.

Research and Development
List of research and development projects
Progress reports of projects
Detail specifications
Cost of development
Patentable ideas

Strategic Planning
Diversification plans
Financial plans
Planned acquisitions
New product direction

Privacy
Equal opportunity plans
Personnel information
Hiring information
Payroll information
Sickness and accident records

Defense Plans

Obviously, many business enterprises — small and large, national and multinational — have information that falls into one or more of these categories. Most government organizations have information, such as defense information, that must be protected. Most of the concepts and controls discussed here are equally applicable to the issue of privacy — protecting information related to employees — as they are to the organization's proprietary information. The issue of privacy is a growing concern, and privacy legislation will probably and eventually require many of the controls discussed in this handbook.

The threats to information security vary in significance. A multinational organization may be concerned about a foreign power's taking over one of its subsidiaries, while a local carpet store may be concerned about keeping sale prices secret until they are advertised. This handbook provides helpful security information for diverse organizations.

Complexity

As stated previously, information security is a complex subject in today's environment. Some organizations have added professional intellectual security staffs to deal with the problem. Chapter 2 explains the need for such staffs and what the responsibilities are. The intellectual security function, while perhaps part of overall security, contrasts sharply with the traditional guard force, both in terms of job skill and stature within the corporation. Some companies are hiring top professionals from governmental law enforcement agencies to deal with the problem.

Information security requires an information-classification system and various levels of protection that could range from locks and keys to encryption. Data security, the protection of information in a computer environment, is a new subject area to which Chapter 5 is devoted.

Information security and how to conduct an information-security audit are equally complex subjects. Auditing information security, along with some recommended approaches, is covered in Chapter 6. Chapter 6 is applicable to management in the implementation and self-review of information security as well as to auditors. Chapter 6 also presents the concept of selective information security as an audit approach and as a technique for maximizing the return on the resources devoted to information security.

Summary

Information security is an important business problem today. A relatively new area where technology is growing by leaps and bounds, it requires innovative security controls. The dynamics of information security require a comprehensive and ongoing information-security program supported by executive management. Up to now, the internal audit profession has not been as actively involved in information security as it has been in other traditional control areas.

The internal auditor must help management ensure that its confidential information is protected. An information-security audit may be an organization's most important audit. If the organization is a commercial enterprise, such an audit may prevent the company from going out of business.

This handbook presents an analysis of information-security exposures and discusses alternative controls, solutions, and audit approaches. It also includes checklists and recommended audit techniques which can be tailored to an organization's environment.

2

The Information-Security Organization

The accomplishment of any objective in business today depends on the proper assignment of responsibility. Properly assigning responsibility and informing employees as to what their responsibilities are in regard to information security is no different from assigning responsibilities for any other business objective. *Every* employee in a company is responsible for information to some degree: basic, primary, and/or ultimate.

All employees have a *basic responsibility* to comply with a company's information-security rules and regulations. For example, all employees should lock their desks, wear badges, and challenge anyone who attempts to enter the building without proper identification.

The *primary responsibility* for information security rests with the originators and proprietors of classified information and with their management. It is the originator who is most knowledgeable about the value of that information to the company and is, therefore, responsible for classifying the information properly and ensuring that only employees with an authorized need to know have access to it. The proprietor is responsible for safeguarding the information until it is destroyed, declassified, or returned to the originator. Because both the originator and the proprietor play such important roles in information security, they have primary responsibility.

Originators and proprietors of classified information are often specialists in one function such as finance or marketing. Although they have primary responsibility for information security, this is not their main function. As a result, they are not experts in security. Therefore, they need a knowledgeable source to guide them and to answer such questions as: What should be classified top priority? What is secure? What procedures should be followed? What are the legal implications? What are the best alternatives?

Also, because of today's need to create and transmit information rapidly, classified information is frequently out of their hands. It passes through the hands of service departments: the typing pool, the reproduction department, the computer center, the graphics department, the audiovisual department, and the mail room. What procedures should these service departments follow, and how can the employees having the primary responsibility for information security be assured that the information is secure while being processed?

All employees should support and commit themselves to their company's information-security plan. They should understand why the company places emphasis on information security and, at the very least, follow rules and regulations.

Whenever an objective involves more than one person, someone must be assigned the *ultimate responsibility* for providing leadership and coordination. Because an effective information-security program does involve every level of the organization, including executive management, a corresponding security organization with ultimate responsibility for the security of classified information must also exist.

Most large corporations have a department, or at least a representative, at every level responsible for personnel. The need for a separate security organization is no different, nor any less important. In fact, a company's future may actually depend on how it faces up to its ultimate responsibility for information security.

Because the security organization has the ultimate responsibility of providing the emphasis, direction, coordination, and education necessary for an effective information-security program, a brief overview of how such an organization should be structured and what its specific mission should include is necessary.

It should be noted that, while the information-security organization has ultimate responsibility, this in no way mitigates management's responsibility. Managers of departments originating or possessing sensitive information have the primary responsibility for protection and must be held accountable for any security deficiencies or breaches.

The Information-Security Organization Model

Because information security is subject to variables such as the type of data processing equipment, the nature of the company's product, and the aggressiveness of the competition, there can be no standard approach to an information-security organization. Each company's individual needs and requirements determine the size, structure, chain of command, and responsibilities. The information-security organization shown in Figure 1 applies equally to large or small organizations. The execution of the responsibilities will be the same in smaller organizations. The only difference is that fewer employees are required to complete the tasks in smaller companies. Security functions can range from being assigned as a portion of one employee's job to requiring a complete department. A security organization model need not be identical to the one shown, but it should have the same components.

Figure 1
Model of Information-Security Staff Organization

The organization as depicted in Figure 1 does not necessarily require direct-line reporting. The information-security officer at location B might report directly to executive management at that location and have dotted-line responsibility to the manufacturing division security staff, for example. Similarly, the finance security representative might report to the controller at location B and have dotted-line responsibility to the location security department.

The organization of information security as discussed here should not be confused with the responsibilities of a guard force: locking doors, monitoring closed-circuit television systems, and performing after-hours tours. Guard-force duties are an integral but small part of a total information-security program.

Corporate Information-Security Officer

The corporate information-security officer sets the direction of security for the entire company. This task cannot be accomplished by writing corporate directives, distributing them throughout the company, and assigning individual groups to review various locations for compliance. This procedure may work for other functions such as finance, but it will not create an effective information-security program for three reasons:

First, no single set of directives can blanket all the areas of information security. The security precautions needed in a research and development division differ significantly from those needed in a manufacturing division. Stringent mandates which afford appropriate security in the former will probably be impractical and unrealistic in the latter. They may, in fact, cause manufacturing personnel to circumvent security procedures and inadvertently create information-security exposures. To be effective, information-security procedures must be custom tailored to each division, to each location, and within each function at that location.

Second, information security is subject to dynamic changes. New and different products being developed require different information-security precautions: as new media are developed for transmitting information, new security precautions become necessary. Therefore, any set of rules made today may not be applicable tomorrow. Each division, location, and function within a location must have the flexibility to adapt security procedures readily.

Third, a group such as internal audit may review the security program at a location only once every two years. What happens in the interim?

Information-security needs are subject to dynamic change. Different functions require varying degrees of security; there cannot be one all-encompassing procedure to ensure an effective security program. The corporate information-security staff should write procedures to cover all aspects of information security, but these should be guidelines only. Such guidelines should state objectives and give possible alternatives for accomplishing them. It would then be the job of the divisional and location information-security people to implement what is best for their particular purposes.

However, certain aspects of information security, such as the information classification system and the distribution system for top-priority material, must be consistent throughout the company. The corporate information-security officer should determine when procedures should be *guidelines* and when they should be *directives.*

After developing security procedures, the corporate information-security function should continue to advise and counsel all levels of management on keeping the procedures current, making major policy decisions that affect the entire company, and investigating any potential breaches of information security.

It is important to note that, while the ultimate responsibility for corporate information security is a staff function, the staff is not responsible for implementing the necessary controls. It is responsible strictly for seeing that an effective information-security program is implemented and for monitoring the program for executive management. It provides technical direction and leadership; operating management at a location is responsible for implementation.

Divisional Information-Security Officer

Divisional information-security officers have the same basic responsibilities as corporate information-security officers but at the division level. They ensure that an effective information-security program is in place at every location within their division and that the location's security programs accomplish corporate objectives. A location's security procedures are determined by the location's function. In a manufacturing division which solely manufactures products sold on the open market, there will be fewer security exposures than in a research and development division which is experimenting with unannounced products. Therefore, each divisional security staff is responsible for defining its specific security exposures and implementing the necessary controls. This may require rewriting corporate security guidelines in more specific and detailed terms, or it may mean just making recommendations within the division. In effect, the divisional security staff interprets corporate procedures and implements effective and plausible security measures for the division.

Location Information-Security Officer

A location information-security department ensures that both divisional and corporate security procedures are properly implemented at its location. At this level, implementing information security becomes more than just a matter of writing procedures. It's a job of ensuring that all functions fulfill their basic and primary responsibilities for security. How can any one person, or even a small group of people, be knowledgeable enough about all the aspects of a business to ensure that all exposures to loss of information have been eliminated?

In truth, a great deal of technical knowledge is not required to accomplish this. A security department accomplishes its mission by ensuring that each function has properly identified its proprietary information. Then, it works hand in hand with functional management to implement the proper security controls to prevent loss.

If, for example, a new product is being developed, a security department will have no technical knowledge about that product nor of the critical components or new technologies involved. The security department would, therefore, ask management charged with developing this product to identify the critical components and technologies. Then it would prepare a comprehensive security plan identifying the critical components and stating how classified information about the product is to be protected.

The information-security function would also help management develop the security plan. In this way, information-security's knowledge of security and technical management's knowledge of a particular product combine to provide the most effective security plan for the new product.

The information-security function is also responsible for ensuring that all employees understand their basic responsibility for security. This can be accomplished through education. The security department can show security films or prepare a special brochure on security rules and regulations. It is important to stress employees' responsibility for security because, without the commitment of all employees, information security cannot exist.

Employees usually have negative reactions to security measures. Security precautions require extra steps which often cause inconvenience and tend to hamper task performance. Consequently, security procedures must be meaningful, and their importance must be understood by the people who are to abide by them. Otherwise, they won't be followed. The security department, working with location management to develop functional security plans, must create an effective overall information-security program to balance the need for security with the need for getting the job done.

Information-Security Representatives

Functional management must assign some special personnel to ensure that all classified information is adequately protected. For this reason, each function should have an information-security representative to work with the security department to develop functional security plans and to ensure that no security risks exist within that function. Security representatives must have a comprehensive knowledge of the function being represented; however, the job of security representative would probably not require the full-time efforts of an employee.

The following quotation from one company summarizes the need for security representatives.

> As time went on, it developed that these security representatives became an important link in the liaison between the security departments and the areas they represented. Through their involvement, we achieved management involvement. Motivation seems to stem from self-preservation.[6]

New Design

New design, an important area that is all too often overlooked, must involve the information-security function. This includes the design of new products, new buildings, or new computer programs. Although the primary responsibility of ensuring that

---

[6] Defense Industrial Security Institute, "Outline of a Space Contractor's Self-Inspection Program" (Orlando, FL: Martin Marietta Corporation, Aerospace Division, May 1973).

information security is built into any new design rests with responsible line management, the information-security staff must adequately define information-security needs. The information-security function can play an independent role and provide helpful advice and counsel to line management.

Involving the information-security staff in new design precludes the development of significant security exposures that may prove too costly to resolve. Further, where proprietary information is involved, information-security personnel should also be involved in major renovations, repairs, or enhancements.

Summary

Information security involves each and every employee within a company. Information security is subject to dynamic change and information-security plans must be tailored to individual functions and even individual departments to meet the needs. A company cannot have an effective information-security program unless it has a vital information-security organization keeping pace and responding to changing security needs.

Only through the welding of the information-security organization, management, and all employees can an effective information-security program exist. The information-security organization's knowledge of security, management's technical knowledge, and the efforts of all employees are the necessary components for information security.

The information-security organization is the focal point for any independent review of information security. Whether a company's information is secure depends on how the security organization faces up to its ultimate responsibility. Therefore, an independent review of information security must include an analysis of how the security organization is structured and how each segment of it is performing. The saying "A chain is only as strong as its weakest link" aptly applies to the information-security organization.

Checklist 1
Information-Security Organization

☐ 1. Does an information-security function exist at all the appropriate levels within the organization: corporate? division? location? functional representatives?

☐ 2. Has the level of involvement of the information-security function been determined by questioning management in other functions?

☐ 3. Has the information-security function interpreted the organization's information-security objectives and developed specific, written guidelines and procedures for the various areas of responsibility?

☐ 4. Has the information-security organization acquired and reviewed functional information-security plans?

☐ 5. Is the information-security function adequately staffed in both personnel and skill requirements?

☐ 6. If necessary, has the responsibility for data processing security been assigned?

☐ 7. Does the information-security officer have the support of executive management?

☐ 8. Has the information-security function created employee awareness of the need for information security through education, posters, newsletters, and other means?

☐ 9. Has the information-security function done an effective job of monitoring the functions it is responsible for and of keeping executive management aware of the status of the information-security program?

☐ 10. Does the information-security function conduct periodic self-reviews? Does it have documented and comprehensive action plans to resolve known security exposures?

☐ 11. Do the action plans include documented assignment of responsibility and target dates?

☐ 12. Are the target dates being met?

☐ 13. Is the information-security staff involved in the design of new buildings, new products, and computer programs?

3

Identification and Classification of Proprietary Information

To keep proprietary information secure, the information must be identified and classified so those who come in contact with it know its importance. Then it must be protected until it is destroyed or no longer proprietary. These constitute three key ingredients of an information-security program: identification, classification, and protection.

An organization's information-security program is based on its identification and classification system and requires the involvement of all employees. It is, therefore, extremely important that everyone in the organization clearly understand the identification and classification system.

Selective Identification of Information: A New Concept

Not all information generated by a company requires safeguarding. In fact, most of it does *not*. Also, all proprietary information is not of *equal value*. The higher its value, however, the more stringent are the security controls necessary to protect it. Therefore, the proper identification of proprietary information and its value to the organization is the foundation of an effective information-security program.

Traditional security measures may be inadequate to protect a company's most valuable information. On the other hand, locking up everything of importance or giving all important information the highest level of classification may interfere with the efficient conduct of business; and the resultant cost may be prohibitive. Overly restrictive and unreasonable policies can undermine the creditability of the entire information-security program.

As stated in Chapter 1, an effective information-security program must provide protection for proprietary information at a reasonable cost. Management needs some way to ensure that the most valuable information is properly protected and that the resources devoted to information security are being used in the most productive manner.

The selective identification and protection of information provides a simple and logical solution. This new technique has four steps:
1. Identify the most valuable information.
2. Evaluate and prioritize it.
3. Understand the use of this key information.
4. Develop a documented information-security plan.

Steps 1 and 2 will be discussed in this chapter. Steps 3 and 4 will be discussed in Chapter 4. The selective identification and protection approach to information security concentrates the resources on the most valuable information while maintaining a reasonable level of controls over less important information.

The First Step: Identifying Valuable Information

The proper identification of the most valuable assets requires the involvement of executive management. Executive management must direct and guide its management teams in identifying the information that requires maximum security attention. The process must involve *all* the activities of that organization and should start with an inventory of information.

In identifying an inventory of information, one important point is that information does not reside only in document form. Parts or prototypes that can be reverse-engineered are also sources to consider in the selective identification process.

This process varies, depending on the characteristics and size of the organization and the functions within it. To be effective, the process must be formal; the scope of activities and the results should be documented and reviewed with executive management. All functions within an organization should demonstrate to both executive management and the internal auditor that they have selectively identified their most valuable information.

Some of the questions to ask during the selective identification of information process are:

What does the information represent? a new direction? a new solution to a technical problem?

Does it contain something unique?

Does it describe an advanced concept?

Does it offer a cost advantage or increased manufacturing capability?

Would it be valuable to a competitor?

How would it impact the organization if the information got into the hands of an unauthorized recipient?

During the selective identification process, care must be taken to determine exactly what is vital about a particular piece of information. The value of information is sometimes contained in only one or two segments of the total information package; and without these vital segments, the information is not valuable. For example, the uniqueness of a new product design may reside in a single algorithm; without this algorithm, the design specifications may be of no value to the competition.

The local security function should coordinate the selective identification of information process to ensure its consistency and effectiveness.

The Second Step: Prioritizing the Information

After key information is identified, it must be ranked in order of importance so information-security resources can be expended where they are most needed. Some information may have a tremendous value to one organization and no value whatever to the competition. Therefore, it would not require protection.

For example, a company may have a tremendous investment in a product test system that is indispensable to it but worthless to another organization because it is specifically tailored to that particular product and its manufacturing process.

By evaluating the relative worth of key information and ranking the information accordingly, an organization can allocate its information-security resources in the most productive manner.

Classification

Communicating the value of information to those who work with it is an important part of the overall information-security program. This is accomplished with a classification system; the primary objective of which is to establish a framework for categorizing information and defining the minimal levels of protection for each category. As previously stated, there are varying levels of proprietary information. The more important the information, the more stringent are the safeguards required to protect it.

It would be reasonable to lock a weekly payroll register in a filing cabinet accessible to all the employees in the payroll department, for instance. However, it would not be reasonable to lock the complete compilation of design specifications for a new product in a similar cabinet accessible to the entire new product design department. New product design specifications should be compartmentalized, and access to the complete compilation limited to the fewest-possible employees. Giving a document that contains all the new product design specifications a higher classification than each of its components will ensure that it receives more protection. Classification identifies the value of information and establishes the minimum level of protection required to protect it.

Employees must understand the information classification system; erroneous classification can have a negative effect on information security. Obviously, if a document is underclassified, it will not be given the necessary protection. However, the over-classification of documents can also adversely affect information security.

Overclassification

The higher the classification, the more rigid are the controls and procedures set forth to protect the information. If information is overclassified, the need for security precautions will not make sense, and employees will tend to ignore the security precautions required for that information. In time, the security precautions required for all information in that classification will be ignored, leaving the appropriately classified information vulnerable. Overclassification results in watering down the attitudes and actions of employees relative to their treatment of classified information.

Also, the higher the security classification, the lower the amount of information that should fall into the category. Over-classification will dilute security because of the volume of information alone.

A Classification System

The classification system discussed here is patterned after the United States Department of Defense procedures. The definitions are taken from the Department of Defense's *Industrial Security Manual for Safeguarding Classified Information.* They have been adapted to fit the needs of business. The reader should refer to this government manual for further information.

Unclassified

Information that can be disclosed without detriment to the organization.[7]

Unclassified indicates that the person who classified the information made a conscious decision about its value. When information has no classification, there is no evidence that such a decision was made; it cannot be determined whether the lack of classification was an oversight. However, when all information requires a classification label, even if that label is unclassified, there is the assurance that a conscious decision was made.

"Unclassified" on the request forms for information ensures that the kind of information sought is communicated to the information service department.

---

[7] U.S. Department of Defense, *Industrial Security Manual For Safeguarding Classified Information* (Alexandria, Virginia: Defense Supply Agency, 1970), p. 3.

Confidential

Information and material, the unauthorized disclosure of which could be detrimental to the best interest of the organization.[8]

This, the lowest classification, is used for information which should not be distributed outside the company. Information in this classification — such as telephone directories and organizational charts — generally has a large distribution inside the company. Its unauthorized disclosure would not seriously damage the company or an employee, but its nature should limit its use to company employees. It is this information, however, that need not be kept under lock and key.

Priority

Information or material, the unauthorized disclosure of which could result in serious damage to a person or to the organization such as by jeopardizing an employee's relations with others, endangering the effectiveness of a program or policy of vital importance to the organization, or compromising important new product plans, scientific or technological developments important to the organization's future.[9]

Most proprietary information will fall into this category and include such documents as personnel records, financial information, payroll information, and engineering drawings of parts to be included in a new product. Information in this category generally has limited distribution within the company. Priority information must be kept under lock and key when not in use and should only be distributed to those employees with an authorized need to know.

Top Priority

Information or material, the security aspect of which is paramount; and the unauthorized disclosure of which could result in exceptionally grave damage to the organization such as allowing the competition to determine the complete details about a future product or compromising the scientific or technological developments vital to the future of the organization.[10]

Examples in this category are complete and comprehensive new product plans, financial operating plans for the future, information describing trade secrets, or a working prototype of a new and unannounced product. The difference between priority and top-priority information may only be one of completeness. The

---

[8] *Ibid.*
[9] *Ibid.*
[10] *Ibid.*

engineering schematics for a new product might be classified priority because they are geographically dispersed and the loss of any single drawing would not give the competition sufficient information to build a similar product. However, any document containing all the engineering drawings for the new product might be classified top priority because it contains all the information to build the product. The top-priority classification is used for information that describes a significant part of a company's ventures and, therefore, requires strict accountability. The procedures to protect top-priority information are presented in Chapter 4.

Compartmentalization

When classifying information, compartmentalization is an effective technique to consider. Often one specific item of valuable information can be isolated, making the remainder of the information less valuable. Also, as mentioned previously, individual components of a new product design specification have less value than the complete compilation. By compartmentalizing information and limiting access to each compartment to those individuals with an absolute need to know, information can be given a lower classification and, thus, require fewer resources to protect it.

Compartmentalization can be defined as *separating information into components to lower classification levels.* Compartmentalization, therefore, reduces security requirements, making it easier to work with the information at lower classification levels.

Legal Implications

A secondary objective of the classification system is to make legal action possible in the event information is misappropriated. In one trade-secret case, *Motorola, Inc., v. Fairchild Camera and Instrument Corp.* (366F. suppl. 1173 D. Arizona, 1973), it was determined that identification of trade secrets is an essential part of an information-security program. To recover damages in a lawsuit, it is generally required that an organization be able to show that the information was valuable, that individuals who came in contact with the information understood its proprietary nature, and that effective precautions were taken to safeguard the information. An information-security classification system can become an important ingredient in litigation.

Obviously, an ineffective classification system might preclude legal recourse if misappropriated information were not listed as highly proprietary.

Summary

Identifying and classifying proprietary information properly is not a simple task. The classification must be based on the answer to the question: What will the consequences be if the information is divulged outside the organization? The more serious they would be, the more important the information becomes. Sometimes information is underclassified because it is technical, involving symbols or figures which the originator assumes will not make sense to others. It must always be assumed that the information will make sense to a perpetrator. If information is classified at a level that requires users to sign for it, they will be less likely to try to steal it.

An important point in classifying information is that the classification category determines how much protection the information will be afforded. The information security staff should prepare minimal levels of information-security requirements for each classification level as well as instructions on how to classify information properly. Adhering to the "selective identification of information" technique ensures proper identification and classification.

Checklist 2:
Classification of Information

☐ 1. Is executive management involved in identifying and classifying information?

☐ 2. Are the organization's instructions regarding information identification and classification of proprietary information presented clearly?

☐ 3. Did the information-security function coordinate the selective identification and prioritization of information?

☐ 4. Sample several functions that are likely to have highly classified information. Can these functions demonstrate that they selectively identified and prioritized their information?

☐ 5. Do these functions have information that, in your opinion, is over- or underclassified?

☐ 6. Have any functions classified their information in only one category?

☐ 7. Question employees. Do they understand the classification program?

☐ 8. Is its application consistent across the organization or facility?

☐ 9. Select a representative sample of classified information. Is it externally labeled with its classification?

☐ 10. Is the unclassified designation used to ensure a conscious classification decision was made for all information?

☐ 11. Did management consider prototypes, parts, or special chemicals in identifying and classifying information?

☐ 12. Has management used the compartmentalization technique to protect the vital information with the least expenditure of resources?

☐ 13. Select key information that has been identified and review the security protection it is being given.

4

Protection

Absolute security is not attainable; in fact, absolute security equals zero productivity. Information is created by people and for people. Until a foolproof method is developed to remove temptation and all people become honest, there is no absolute way to guard against information-security breaches.

The closest thing to absolute security is a system like the ones used by maximum security prisons or top-secret government installations. Under these, all employees are fingerprinted, investigated, and physically searched upon entering and leaving buildings. But even with these rigid security controls, prisoners still escape and top-secret information is leaked. If someone wants the information badly enough to take the necessary risks and devises a plan to obtain it, he or she will probably be successful in getting it.

Most of us, especially those in management, would agree that prison-like environments or the rigid security of top-secret government installations is impractical, unrealistic, and uneconomical in business. The security procedures and controls to be presented here are not expected to accomplish absolute security. However, there are five specific objectives that can ensure that information-security technology is compatible with information-processing technology.

These objectives are (1) limiting the number of people who have access to classified information, (2) increasing the risk of being caught — a significant deterrent by itself, (3) setting the legal groundwork for prosecution and payment for damages in the event of a security breach, (4) providing an audit trail to identify who had access to classified information, and (5) ensuring that any loss of classified information will not go undetected. With knowledge about the loss of classified information, action can be taken to preclude some of the possible consequences.

The protection of classified information requires a number of controls and protection techniques:
1. selective protection of information (third and fourth steps)
2. quantitative risk analysis and evaluation technique
3. traditional controls: locks, fences, guards
4. islands of security
5. information-service functions
6. top-priority document control
7. new product-security plans

8. trade-secret security
9. intellectual security
10. destruction

Selective Protection of Information
The Third Step: Determining How the Information Is Used
After an organization identifies and assigns priorities to its vital information, it must determine how, where, and by whom the information is to be used. The simplest and most effective way to reduce risk is to restrict the number of employees who have access to those with an authentic need to know or a need to use.

The Fourth Step: Developing an Information-Security Plan
Once management has identified, assigned priorities to, and determined how proprietary information is to be used, it develops a formal, documented security plan. The plan should achieve the proper balance between information security on the one hand and the need for effective communication and control of costs on the other.

The key to selective information security is tailoring the security-protection program to the particular kind of information rather than basing it on a general set of procedures applicable to all information. Highly classified information will get maximum protection; the remaining proprietary information will have protection consistent with its classification level.

A security program may depend solely on traditional protection mechanisms. It may use new techniques like compartmentalization, or it can combine the old and the new. Operating management is responsible for developing a selective information-protection plan based on good judgment and experience. However, the information-security function should play an active role in defining how to develop such a plan, should monitor its development, and provide advice and counsel. Periodic reviews and audits ensure that the selective protection of information plan is working and giving vital information protection consistent with its value and affording reasonable protection to other proprietary information. It should also assure the best use of information-security resources.

Quantitative Risk Analysis and Evaluation Technique
Determining the security requirements necessary to protect proprietary information and the amount of money to be invested in protection are prime considerations. Before discussing them, a look should be taken at a technique which can be a valuable exercise for management, as well as for the auditor, in putting security requirements into perspective and economically evaluating various protection alternatives. The technique can be implemented subjectively or complemented by another technique which quantifies the amount of risk, assigns priority to the most vulnerable information and

determines which security precaution will effect the greatest risk reduction per dollar invested. The five factors of one such quantitative technique follow:

1. Value
   Estimate the loss to the company if the information is disclosed to an unauthorized recipient. The value of information can be determined by estimating the additional market quantities a competitor will gain by acquiring the information, multiplying the quantity times the unit selling price, and multiplying the result by the profit factor.
2. Probability
   Evaluate the current level of protection afforded the information. Is there a high, medium, low, or minimal probability of unauthorized disclosure? Rate *high* as 4, *medium* as 3, *low* as 2, and *minimal* as 1.
3. Risk
   To obtain the risk factor, multiply the value by the probability.
4. Alternatives
   Determine and compare the risk reduction to the cost of implementing and maintaining alternative security improvements.
5. Selection
   Select the alternative which will yield the greatest reduction in risk per dollar invested.
   The following two examples illustrate the use of this technique.

Example 1: assigning priority to information to be protected

A company has identified as proprietary information a computer program used to design a new product, the actual design drawings, a prototype of a critical component which is subject to reverse engineering, and the potential customer list. It decides to evaluate and improve the security of this information.

It starts by estimating the value of the information.

Computer program	$10 million
Design drawings	$6 million
Prototype	$4 million
Customer list	$3 million

Next it determines the probability of this information being disclosed to an unauthorized individual.

Information	Current Protection	Probability
Computer program	Computer center/strict access control	1, minimal
Design drawings	Top priority/strict accountability	2, low
Prototype	Locked in regular cabinet	4, high
Customer list	Top priority/strict accountability	2, low

Then it computes the risk.

Information	Value	X Probability	= Risk Factor	Priority
Computer Program	$10 million	1	$10 million	3
Design drawings	$ 6 million	2	$12 million	2
Prototype	$ 4 million	4	$16 million	1
Customer list	$ 3 million	2	$ 6 million	4

From the analysis, increasing the security protection of the prototype should be the first priority.

Example 2: selecting the best alternative

The alternatives for increasing protection of the prototype are:

- install a vault (for safekeeping when the prototype is unattended) at a cost of $5,000
- locate personnel working on the prototype within an island of security (restricted access area) and install a vault and motion detectors for after-hours security at a cost of $8,000
- locate personnel working on the prototype within an island of security, install a vault, and hire 24-hour guard service at an original cost of $30,000 with recurring annual costs of $45,000 for salaries

The value of the prototypes in the first example was determined as $4 million. The probability of loss for the various alternatives can be estimated as:

Alternative	Probability
As is	4
A	3
B	2
C	1

The risk factor with the various alternatives is determined by multiplying the value by the probability.

Alternative	Value	X Probability	= Risk Factor
As is	$4 million	4	$16 million
A	$4 million	3	$12 million
B	$4 million	2	$ 8 million
C	$4 million	1	$ 4 million

To compare alternatives, determine the amount of risk reduction that will be obtained per dollar invested.

Alternative	Risk	Risk Reduction	Implementation Cost	Risk Reduction Per $ Invested
As is	$16 million	–N/A	–N/A	–N/A
A	$12 million	$ 4 million	$ 5 thousand	= $ 800
B	$ 8 million	$ 8 million	$ 8 thousand	= $1,000
C	$ 4 million	$12 million	$30 thousand	= $ 400

Without considering recurring costs, it is apparent that alternative B will result in the greatest risk reduction for each dollar invested. However, prior to making the final decision, the impact on the company's total profit must be assessed if the prototype falls into the hands of the competition. Management must determine if the company can afford the additional risk inherent in alternative B as opposed to alternative C.

The dollar-value estimates derived from this technique are not actual; however, the results show the proper relationships and help quantify a company's information-security requirements. A quantitative information-security evaluation technique should be used to ensure that information-security requirements are in proper perspective and whether this technique or one similar is used.

Checklist Number 3:
Selective Protection of Information

☐ 1. Select a representative sample of the most valuable information in the organization.
☐ 2. Is there a documented security plan for this information?
☐ 3. Does the plan take into account the characteristics of the information (who uses it? where and how?)?
☐ 4. Was an attempt made to quantify the information-security exposures and risk reduction?
☐ 5. Have these plans been reviewed and approved by executive management and the information-security function?
☐ 6. Are these plans comprehensive, and do they provide for adequate security?
☐ 7. Has the plan been effectively implemented and tested wherever possible? The answer to this question is the most important part of the audit.

Traditional Security: Locks, Fences, and Guards

The security procedures in this category primarily prevent, or at least delay, unauthorized personnel from accessing company facilities. A location's guard force is generally responsible for implementing most of these procedures.

It is generally accepted that the traditional security controls such as perimeter and after-hours security are psychological deterrents only. A potential perpetrator faced with such obstacles as fences, locked doors, alarms, and guard patrols may see the risk of being caught as being too great and decide not to attempt access. On the other hand, the value of the information to be obtained may make the risks worthwhile.

The loss of sensitive information to nonemployees is not the only security exposure. Although traditional security procedures are an integral part of the total information security plan, they are only one aspect. They must be supplemented with new and more advanced techniques. As one writer states, "Psychological deterrents should not be relied upon for protection of a facility; the tranquility they bring to an owner could prove costly."[11]

Traditional security measures generally include guarded entrances and exits, employee identification, nonpermanent employee

---

[11] Richard J. Healy, *Design for Security* (New York: John Wiley and Sons, Inc., 1968), p. 3.

control, key control, guard duties, design, and organizational and personnel controls.

These traditional security controls are relatively simple and approved by both management and auditors. Internal auditing has been active in reviewing these controls as part of security audits of other physical assets. Therefore, with the exception of a discussion on organizational and personnel controls, only a general checklist outlining these controls is needed here. If further discourse is desired, there are many excellent books on these subjects.

Organizational and Personnel Controls

While organizational and personnel controls are important traditional control areas, they are also the most likely not to be implemented. The employee may be highly trusted. Rotating jobs may disrupt the function. The organization may not be large enough to provide separation of duties. As a result, information-security exposures are created, and employees are often placed in environments that are conducive to theft of information — especially where there are inadequate controls. As stated previously, management has a moral obligation to create an environment reasonably free of temptation. Because organizational and personnel controls are traditional, they will be outlined only briefly in this handbook.

Organizational controls have three major elements. Information-security objectives, as well as such other objectives as increased efficiency, are usually achieved by:
1. separating functions
2. separating duties within functions
3. assigning information-security responsibility

Separating the functions into logical entities, each of which requires different components, is an effective tool for minimizing access to data. In effect, organizational controls result in information compartmentalization which effectively reduces access to data. For example, two unique characteristics of a new product are a prototype and a special chemical. Knowledge of one without knowledge of the other is useless. Organizing one function to be responsible for the prototypes and another for the chemical compartmentalizes the information and restricts access.

The same concept can be accomplished *within* a function as easily as *between functions.* .

Lastly, information-security responsibility must be assigned. The creation of information-security centers is only one step. In addition, everyone in the organization must accept information-security responsibilities and what those responsibilities are must be clearly understood.

The five major elements of good personnel practices to ensure information security are:
1. *hiring practices*   2. *employment practices*

3. *certified acknowledgement*   *4. job rotation*
      5. termination practices
      The objectives of the hiring practices in regard to information security are twofold: employees selected to work in sensitive areas should be thoroughly screened to minimize the possibility of employing a dishonest person; employees hired to perform specific information-security functions should be well qualified.

Employees in key jobs should be paid and treated better than the average in the industry or profession. This lessens the chances of their choosing to work for a competitor and taking valuable information with them. It is also a valuable and effective deterrent to breaches of intellectual security.

Regarding trade secrets, one effective control is to require all employees to sign a business conduct and ethics certification card stating they have read and *understand* their responsibilities to the employer. An annual reminder of this kind can be an excellent deterrent to information security incidents.

Job rotation serves a useful purpose in protecting information in such functions as new product development.

Finally, termination practices must ensure that all proprietary information is returned and that access to the buildings and all data processing services is discontinued. The employee's understanding of responsibilities to the employer should also be obtained in writing at the exit interview. This is extremely important for employees working in sensitive areas.

In summary, management must constantly remember the importance and reliability of organizational and personnel controls.

Legal Implications of Traditional Controls
Traditional security controls will probably not be sufficient to demonstrate that an effective information-security program was in existence if legal recourse has to be sought for a security breach.

> *These measures, although certainly helpful in preventing theft of trade secrets, probably afford protection to all areas of the plant and therefore are of little help in demonstrating the security measures used to protect trade secrets.*[12]

These important areas should be reviewed during an information-security audit; however, a minimal amount of time should be spent on traditional security controls. The internal audit profession must graduate from this level of review and provide management with more comprehensive and sophisticated reviews of the entire information-security program.

---

[12] Op. cit., Practising Law Institute, p. 38.

32

Checklist 4
Traditional Security

Entrances/Exits:

☐ 1. Are authorized entrances during normal working hours limited to the fewest possible number to allow the guard force to maintain control?

☐ 2. Are all other entrances locked?

☐ 3. If entrances are not manned and access is gained by using a magnetic identification badge or other device, have employees been instructed to challenge tailgaters? Do they?

☐ 4. Are shipping and receiving areas designed so that truckers and other vendors cannot gain access to the exterior of the building unless so authorized?

☐ 5. Review the exterior of the building to ensure there are no other possible unsecured entrances such as windows, sidewalk elevators, sewers, and ventilation shafts.

☐ 6. Are only manned entrances/exits used for access to and egress from the building after normal working hours?

☐ 7. Do all other entrances and exits have alarm systems?

☐ 8. Is the wiring for the alarm system concealed to prevent bypassing?

☐ 9. Is the alarm system tested?

☐ 10. Have instructions been issued to employees defining after-hours entrance/exist procedures?

☐ 11. Is exterior lighting adequate?

☐ 12. Is there an auxiliary power source?

☐ 13. Is the use of closed-circuit television necessary to monitor entrances? Is it used? Are there any blind spots?

Employee Identification:

☐ 1. Have badges and identification cards been designed to minimize the possibility of duplication?

☐ 2. Do they contain a photograph of the employee along with his or her name?

☐ 3. Are badges and identification cards serialized for accountability?

☐ 4. Does the issuance of a badge or identification card require an authorized signature (manager or personnel department)?

☐ 5. Are there procedures to ensure that employees leaving the company return their badges and/or identification cards?

☐ 6. Is a record maintained of lost badges and identification cards? Is the employee's manager notified?

☐ 7. If a computerized system is used for allowing entrance to the building, is a lost badge immediately removed from the active file?

☐ 8. Are records maintained indicating the serial numbers of badges

and their disposition (for example, issued to John Doe, lost, destroyed, unissued)?
- [ ] 9. Are unissued badges and identification cards kept secure?
- [ ] 10. Are periodic inventories taken to ensure that no unissued badges have been lost or stolen?
- [ ] 11. Is the list of active badges or identification cards periodically compared to personnel files to determine if employees who have left the company failed to return their badges or identification cards? Is follow-up action taken?
- [ ] 12. Are employees wearing badges at all times when they are in the building?
- [ ] 13. Have employees been instructed to challenge people not displaying badges within the building? Do they?

Nonpermanent Employee and Visitor Control:
- [ ] 1. Are contractors and other vendors required to enter and leave the building through a single manned entrance?
- [ ] 2. Are they issued badges on a daily basis only? Do the badges clearly identify them as contractors?
- [ ] 3. Is the date for which the badge is valid shown on the badge? Contractor badges should not be designed to allow entrance through unmanned doors.
- [ ] 4. Have identities and reasons for entrance been determined?
- [ ] 5. Are they required to sign in and out?
- [ ] 6. Are they met by supervisory personnel and escorted? If they must access areas within the building where classified information is kept, are they supervised at all times?
- [ ] 7. If they need to gain entrance through other doors to bring in materials and supplies, are they escorted?
- [ ] 8. Is temporary help used only for jobs where access to classified information is neither necessary nor possible (for example, temporary employees should not perform guard duties)?
- [ ] 9. Do badges issued to temporary help identify them as such?
- [ ] 10. Do the badges have an expiration date?
- [ ] 11. Are visitors required to sign in and out?
- [ ] 12. Are they issued badges identifying them as such?
- [ ] 13. Are they met in the lobby and escorted at all times?
- [ ] 14. Are the badges returned when they leave?

Key Control:
- [ ] 1. Is the issuance of keys controlled by a central group (guard force)?
- [ ] 2. Is a system of master and submaster keys used?
- [ ] 3. Are the procedures for key issuance adequate?
  - Are keys issued to only those individuals designated by management who have a need?

- Do key records include name, department, and data?
- Are records kept up-to-date?
- Is the issuance of master and submaster keys limited to a few individuals with an absolute need? Is their need periodically reviewed?
- Is the loan of all keys, particularly master and submaster keys, to personnel on a need basis controlled (for example, guards and maintenance)? Is a register kept? If keys are not returned, is immediate follow-up action taken?

☐ 4. Are investigations conducted to locate lost keys?
☐ 5. If keys are lost, is the lock changed?

Guard Duties:

☐ 1. Is the guard force up to authorized head count?
☐ 2. Do the selection criteria for guards include physical condition, age, mental attitude, education, and background?
☐ 3. Is the salary level high enough to attract qualified individuals?
☐ 4. Are the guards given sufficient training?
☐ 5. Review the location of guard posts and punch-the-clock stations. Do guard tours provide adequate surveillance of classified areas? Frequencies and routes of guard tours should be varied so that an identifiable pattern does not develop.
☐ 6. Do guards issue security violations (for such things as unlocked desks and leaving priority or top-priority material out)?
☐ 7. Are classified areas well lighted to facilitate thorough checking by the guards?
☐ 8. Is there an after-hours guard control station?
☐ 9. Are there procedures identifying what should be done in the event of a security incident? Are they thoroughly understood by the guards?
☐ 10. Do the procedures include current names and phone numbers of executive management, local police, or other governmental agencies?
☐ 11. Is there a two-way communication system between the roving guards and the control station?
☐ 12. Are the guards required to check in periodically?
☐ 13. Are car patrols used?

Organization and Personnel Controls:

☐ 1. Is access to highly proprietary information separated *between* functions and *within* functions as appropriate?
☐ 2. Is information-security responsibility clearly assigned?
☐ 3. Do hiring practices ensure that employees placed in highly sensitive positions are screened? that information-security positions are filled by qualified candidates?
☐ 4. Are employment practices adequate to ensure better-than-average treatment of people in highly sensitive positions?

□ 5. Is employee certification of knowledge of information-security responsibilities obtained in writing?

□ 6. Are key jobs from an information-security standpoint rotated frequently?

□ 7. Do personnel-termination practices and intercompany-transfer practices ensure that employees' access to proprietary data is discontinued?

Islands of Security

Islands of security, restricted access areas within a building, serve two purposes. During normal working hours, they keep unauthorized employees from having access to classified information; after working hours they serve as an added obstacle or deterrent to an intruder.

The security required for each island depends on the classification of the information housed within it. A department involved with developing trade secrets may be housed within an island of security which requires special identification procedures to enter and is equipped with a motion detection device for after-hours surveillance. The secretarial pool may require only that its entrance be locked after hours. Possible security procedures are in Checklist 5. The auditor must determine what functions should be housed within an island of security and whether the security procedures taken for each island are consistent with the security needs of the information housed there.

Some functions requiring housing within an island of security are:

trade secrets	legal
new products development	mail room
top-priority document control	graphics
information service groups	audiovisual communications
finance	record storage
personnel	reproductions
computer installation	secretarial services

Checklist 5
Islands of Security

The auditor should review the information-security exposures possible in specific functions and determine whether they should be housed within an island of security. The following questions pertain to the security precautions and the level of security which must be maintained for each island.

□ 1. Is access restricted at all times to personnel authorized by management?

□ 2. Is a current list of authorized personnel maintained by management?

☐ 3. Have control procedures been established for visitors (including unauthorized employees)? Do the visitors require escorting?

☐ 4. Are electronic alarms or other detection devices used during periods when *no one* should be in the area?

☐ 5. Are these alarms and devices hooked up to the guard's central control station?

☐ 6. Are they periodically tested?

☐ 7. Is closed-circuit TV surveillance of the area necessary?

☐ 8. Have procedures for cleaning of restricted areas been reviewed?

☐ 9. Are cleaners escorted?

☐ 10. Has the admittance system been reviewed?

- If badge system, are the badges color-coded to designate authorized access to that area?
- Are badges for that area issued only upon management authorization?
- If badges are issued by a central group, such as the guard force, is a list of people possessing these badges periodically sent to management for review?
- Are there procedures to ensure the return of badges when an employee leaves the function?
- If access to an area is obtained through doors supplied with combination locks, are the combinations changed periodically?
- Are the combinations changed automatically when an employee leaves the function?
- How is a new combination disseminated to authorized employees?
- If access is gained by keys, who has the keys? Is there effective control of the keys?

Information Service Functions

Within an organization, there are a number of administrative functions, other than the computer center, which process information. A partial list would include:

audiovisual communications	mail room
employee communications	record storage
external communications	reproductions
graphics	secretarial services
keypunch	teletypes and telecopiers

Because the information is out of the owner's control when being created, reproduced, or distributed by these functions, there must be security procedures to ensure that the information does not get lost while being processed. Each of these information service groups must have established security procedures consistent with the classification of the information processed. The location's security department should approve these security plans.

Checklist 6
Information Service Functions
Section 1 refers to general security procedures which apply to most functions. The remaining sections refer to special security requirements related to a specific function.

☐ 1. General
- Does each service organization have information-security procedures that have been approved by the security department? Are they being followed?
- Is the service function housed within an island of security? Review the security of this area (refer to Checklist 5).
- Do only permanent employees handle priority information?
- Does the function label completed information with the appropriate classification (letters, slides, movies, artwork, charts, and storage boxes)? This does not apply to employee communications, external communication, mail room or reproductions.
- Are lockable cabinets provided for the storage of priority information during nonworking hours?
- Is priority information given only to authorized recipient? (Priority information should not be placed in self-service, pickup areas.)
- Are locked containers conveniently available for the disposal of priority information?
- Where applicable, does the request for service forms require indicating the information's classification? The requestor should have to indicate whether the information is priority, confidential, or unclassified. In this way, the service function can give the information the required security protection, label it properly, and ensure that the requestor made a conscious decision as to the classification.
- When it is necessary to send information to a vendor for processing, is a nondisclosure agreement on file for the vendor? A standard agreement form should be developed by the legal department.
- Is the requestor aware that this information will be processed by a vendor?
- Whenever possible, is only unclassified information sent out for vendor's processing?
- When a third-party delivery service is used, is priority information shipped in locked containers?

☐ 2. Audiovisual Communications

- Is the production of movies, slide presentations, or videotapes authorized in advance by management?
- Does management review the final product to ensure that priority information is not included unless so authorized?

☐ 3. Employee Communications
- Review the approval cycle for articles which are to appear in employee media (such as newsletters and bulletins).
- Are all articles approved prior to print?
- Are articles relating to specific functions referred to appropriate management for approval?

☐ 4. External Communications
- Is there one function responsible for coordinating and ensuring that all communications to be released outside the company are properly approved? This includes answering the telephone; news releases; the publishing of articles, theses, or books by employees; and talks by employees to outside organizations.
- Have procedures been written specifying the person or the function to approve specific subject matter? (financial information approved by the controller, for example.)

☐ 5. Mail room
- Is each department provided with a locked mail box?
- What precautions are taken for mail held in the mail room during nonworking hours?

☐ 6. Record Storage
     This includes records held in a central storage area on site due to legal or other retention requirements and records held off site as vital record backup in the event of disaster.
- Review the procedure for delivery of records from the departments to the storage area. Is adequate security provided?
- How are priority documents identified?
- What controls exist over who may request that records be returned from storage?
- Is there follow-up to ensure the return of records withdrawn from storage?
- How are classified records disposed of when they reach their expiration date?

☐ 7. Reproductions
- Are central manned-reproduction service areas used?
- Does the reproduction of a priority document require a manager's signature?
- Have employees of the reproduction center been instructed not to reproduce top-priority information unless requested by the top-priority document control center?
- Are all copiers secured after hours? After-hour requests

should be controlled by the guard force.
- ☐ 8. Secretarial Services
  - ● Have secretaries been instructed to destroy or secure magnetic cards, magnetic tapes, or ribbons used in the creation of priority information?
- ☐ 9. Teletype and Telecopier
  - ● Is priority information sealed in an envelope and delivered only to the addressee?
  - ● Are security controls for the transmission and receiving of priority information through teletype and teleprocessor reviewed?

Top-Priority Document Control

The security of top-priority information requires strict accountability at all times. To ensure consistency and to establish organization-wide control when documents are distributed between locations, there must be a top-priority document control system. The system should include top-priority document control centers at each location and specific procedures for the creation, identification, storage, distribution, and destruction of top-priority information.

Accountability requires that top-priority information be transferred only between control centers. Each control center must keep records of the whereabouts of top-priority information created by that location as well as any that has been received from another location. Control centers can verify that the recipient is authorized, and complete accountability can be maintained. Every top-priority document should have an authorized recipient list. The fewest possible number of people should have access to top-priority documents, and additions to the list must be authorized by the top-priority document originator. The holder of the document can allow other employees to review it; formal authorization is not required.

An audit of information security should include extensive testing of the top-priority document control records to be sure they are accurate and that effective security is being provided.

Checklist 7:
Top-Priority Document Control

- ☐ 1. The originator of a top-priority document should create an authorized access list. This list should be kept to a minimum, and only the originator can authorize access for additional employees.
- ☐ 2. Top-priority documents should have a control number. The central number should be on every page and reflect the originator's location.
- ☐ 3. All copies of top-priority documents should be serialized. Documents can also be individualized by placing the recipient's employee number on each page.

☐ 4. A continuous receipt system should be established for the transmittal of top-priority documents, both within and outside the facility.

☐ 5. The transmittal of top-priority documents between company locations should be from control station to control station. Receipt verification procedures should be established.

☐ 6. Only authorized cabinets should be used for storage of top-priority documents.

☐ 7. Weekly inventories should be taken of all top-priority material. If any documents are missing, the originator should be notified immediately and efforts to trace them begun.

☐ 8. Two people should witness and evidence in writing the destruction of top-priority documents.

☐ 9. Originating management should review documents for possible reclassification annually.

☐ 10. Controls should be established to prevent the unauthorized reproduction of top-priority information.

☐ 11. Controls should be in place to ensure the proper destruction of materials used to create top-priority documents (for example, handwritten notes, dictaphone recordings, ribbons, or magnetic tapes or cards used in typewriters, or carbon paper).

New Product Security Plans

The protection of information related to new products may be the most important aspect of an organization's information-security program. The success of new products determines the future of the company, and their competitive edge in the marketplace determines their success.

The development of any new product requires the generation of information in many forms. Unauthorized disclosure of some essential information may give the competition an edge in the marketplace, while unauthorized disclosure of other information may have no effect whatever on the company.

New products are subject to different security exposures and require different security precautions. The uniqueness of a new product can depend on a new idea, a new technology, a new material or substance, a new process, a new design, or a combination of these. The uniqueness is what gives it the competitive edge, and any information related to its uniqueness demands protection. For one product, this may mean classifying information that is in document form as top priority; for another, whose uniqueness depends on material and process, it may mean maintaining strict accountability of the processed material which is subject to reverse engineering.

Because of the volume of information generated in the development of a new product and because not every new product is subject to the same security exposures, management must develop a new product security plan for each and every new product.

The first step in developing a new product security plan is identifying all the information related to it, no matter what form the information is in. Then the information must be individually assessed to determine what effect its disclosure would have on the success of the new product. The information must be classified appropriately. If information is not in document form like prototypes or material, other security procedures must be implemented.

The new product security plan also determines who has access to the information, whether the new product department should be housed within an island of security, and what level of security is to be maintained within it. After new product management has identified the information, its respective vulnerability, and the security precautions to be afforded it, the security department reviews this preliminary plan, makes recommendations, and finally approves it.

Only by making a conscious and comprehensive effort to evaluate the importance of all information related to a new product and developing a security plan for that product will management be able to identify all the potential security risks and take action to minimize them.

Checklist 8
New Product Security

☐ 1. Review security plans for each new product.
☐ 2. Are they approved by the security department?
☐ 3. Are they being followed?
☐ 4. Are controls in place to safeguard all sensitive information related to the new product?
   Note: Determine what the new products's uniqueness depends upon. If it is design dependent, concentrate on the security of the design specifications. If it is material dependent, concentrate on the accountability of the material. If it is process dependent, concentrate on the precautions taken to protect information documents describing the process. If management has done its job and developed a good security plan, this determination should already have been made.
☐ 5. Is the new product function housed within an island of security?
☐ 6. Is the level of security maintained within the island adequate?

Trade Secrets

Black's *Law Dictionary* defines a trade secret as *a plan or process, tool, mechanism, or compound known only to its owners and those of his employees to whom it is necessary to confide it.*[13]

---

[13] Henry C. Black, *Black's Law Dicitionary* (St. Paul, Minnesota: West Publishing Co., 1951), p. 1666.

Trade secrets generally result from the efforts of a research and development function. During the research and development cycle, an idea will seem worth developing on a larger scale in the hope of perfecting a process, material, or technology that will eventually result in a revolutionary new product or a substantial improvement to a current product. This information becomes a trade secret, for it is extremely valuable to the company.

Research projects should be identified as early as possible as trade secrets to ensure that patent protection is applied for and that other security precautions are implemented. Otherwise, further expenditures in the research and development of the project may be wasted. One method of doing this is to have all research and development departments periodically submit status reports on their projects to a trade-secret review board. This board should have the executive managers of the research and development function and a representative from the legal department. They would evaluate each project for its potential value to the company and determine whether it is patentable.

After a project is identified as a trade secret, a security plan should be developed for all information related to it. The security department should approve the plan just as it does new product security plans.

It may be neither practical nor desirable to classify *all* trade-secret information as top priority. The development of a revolutionary new material may require scientific testing and experimentation by 60 technicians. The rigid security restrictions required would hamper the expedient development of this new material. Often, the security of top-priority information comes from limiting access to it to a few key individuals. In this example, 60 technicians and their managers would have access to information related to the trade secret and the trade-secret material itself, thereby diluting the security normally given to top-priority information. This would necessitate implementing other controls and procedures. Perhaps the information and tasks to be performed by the 60 technicians could be distributed in such a way that no one person would have access to enough information to be able to understand all the processes and ingredients that make up the trade-secret material; or, perhaps, the departments working on the trade secret should reside within separate islands of security.

The auditor should review each trade-secret security plan to ensure there is adequate protection and that the plan is being followed. The auditor should also check with the legal department to ensure that any legal considerations are included in the plan. One legal precaution is ensuring that each employee knows he or she is either working on the development of a trade secret or is using trade-secret-related information. This knowledge should be verified in writing so the employee cannot plead ignorance in the event of a security breach.

Many companies today have new employees sign a statement that they will not disclose sensitive information or use it for personal gain. Although the employees' obligation to the employer may be only implied, it is advisable to have a written agreement — particularly in the case of trade secrets.

> *Even though implied obligation is always present, it is a good idea to have an express agreement to the effect, reduced to writing. This can have the effect of not only preventing an employee from revealing your trade secrets but it will also place upon him the affirmative obligation to disclose to you the trade secrets such as customer lists, formulas, processes, and the like created by him.*[14]

Checklist 9
Trade Secrets

☐ 1. Has a trade-secret review board been established to ensure the timely identification of trade secrets?
☐ 2. Are trade-secret security plans developed and approved by the security department?
☐ 3. Are the procedures being followed?
☐ 4. Is the trade-secret function housed within an island of security?
☐ 5. Is an adequate level of security maintained within?
☐ 6. Is adequate protection being afforded to the trade secret?
☐ 7. Are all employees aware that they are working on a trade secret?
☐ 8. Is this awareness evidenced in writing? Have employees signed a nondisclosure agreement form designed by the legal department?

Intellectual Security

All the structural, mechanical, and administrative information security procedures and controls discussed in this handbook are worthless without the active and willing support of all employees. Information is an expression of human intelligence. It is created by humans for other humans. The employees of an organization create and document the information. They understand its value; they must protect it. Oddly enough, they also pose the biggest threat to loss of information.

Intellectual security, which is an important part of information security, should ensure:

● that employees understand the need for information security and the vital role they play in protecting it

---

[14] *Prentice-Hall Encyclopedic Dictionary of Business Law* (Englewood Cliffs, New Jersey: Prentice-Hall, Inc., 1961), p. 548.

- that employees understand the requirements of the information-security program
- that employees are willing to comply with security regulations and to be on the alert for security deficiencies
- that employees understand their specific responsibilities in regard to proprietary information and that they evidence their understanding in writing
- that employees work in an environment of intellectual honesty so they will not be tempted to misappropriate information

Information security is basically negative. An information-security program includes a list of things not to be done and another list of extra steps which must be taken in task performance. Whenever something is negative, it usually breeds apathy. To overcome this problem and accomplish the objectives, each organization must have a vigorous, ongoing employee security-awareness program. New employees should get information-security orientation; all employees should attend classes reemphasizing security periodically. Educating managers is particularly important because they serve as a continual source of information for employees.

Continuing publicity reminds employees about security. Publicity should use all available media including daily newsletters, bulletin boards, phone books, management letters, enclosures in pay envelopes, and special security pamphlets. Security incidents that occur within the organization or within related organizations should be described to employees as part of their information-security education.

Guards should notify violators. Employees leaving their desks unlocked or losing their badges should be issued violation citations and their supervisors should be informed. The number of security violations should be tracked by function and department. When there appears to be an excessive number in an area, managers should be notified. Also, security should be made an item on employee and management appraisals.

Lastly, a few creative ideas can change security from a negative program to a positive one. Why not give a plaque to the department or function which receives the fewest security violations for the month? A system of awards can also be established for individuals. Many companies are already using award systems to encourage cost effectiveness and safety. Why not security? The awards can range from certificates to gifts like keychains and money clips. Pins with a security emblem can be given to employees who submit ideas for improving security. When an employee's area is found to be secure, why not leave a card with a thank-you message on it?

Continuing emphasis and efforts such as these stimulate employee awareness and result in an effective information-security program. When information security is viewed in a positive rather than a negative vein, employees participate.

Many companies require employees to certify annually that they have read a conduct and ethics guideline clearly defining their responsibilities for information security. This is probably the simplest way to ensure that employees understand their responsibilities to divulge all information learned while working for the organization to the organization and to the organization only. Initial and exit interviews are also good controls in this area.

Management has a responsibility to create an honest working environment for employees. It also has a responsibility to stress in its employee awareness and education programs that violations to procedure or actual misappropriation will not be tolerated and to state the consequences of such actions.

Checklist 10:
Intellectual Security

☐ 1. Are all new employees given a security orientation?
☐ 2. Are periodic refresher classes on security given to *all* employees, particularly managers?
☐ 3. Is an effective publicity campaign in place?
☐ 4. Are all applicable media being used — newsletters, bulletin boards, phone books, management letters, enclosures in pay envelopes, and special security pamphlets?
☐ 5. Are security violation citations issued?
☐ 6. Is the employee's manager notified of violations?
☐ 7. Are violations tracked and monitored by function or department?
☐ 8. Is security included in employee-performance appraisals?
☐ 9. Is part of a manager's performance evaluation based on how well his or her function abides by security rules and regulations?
☐ 10. Are efforts taken to make security a positive rather than a negative program?
☐ 11. Do the employees understand that the need for information security is real?
☐ 12. Do the employees understand the requirements of information-security instructions?
☐ 13. Are employees willing to comply with security regulations?
☐ 14. Do employees document their specific understanding of their information-security responsibilities in writing?
☐ 15. Has management created an environment of "intellectual honesty"?

Destruction

It takes much time, effort, and money to protect classified information while it is in use. These expenditures will be wasted if the information is not adequately destroyed after it has served its useful purpose. The following procedures ensure adequate destruction of classified information.

1. Classified information should be destroyed as soon as it is no longer needed.

2. Locked containers should be conveniently located throughout the building for the disposal of priority documents and such things as typewriter ribbons.

3. These containers should be emptied frequently and the contents immediately destroyed.

4. Information should be destroyed in such a way that it cannot be reconstructed in whole or in part. Acceptable methods of destroying paper products include pulping, pulverizing, shredding, and burning. The destruction of other classified information, such as material or prototypes, can be accomplished by mutilation, pulverization, chemical decomposition, or melting.

5. The destruction of priority information by a vendor or municipality requires the supervision of a company employee.

6. The destruction of top-priority information should be witnessed by two employees of the top-priority center, evidenced in writing, and records of the destruction maintained.

Checklist 11
Information Destruction

☐ 1. Has the location issued procedures regarding the destruction of classified information?

☐ 2. Have the procedures been approved by the security department?

☐ 3. Do they include the requirement to destroy classified information as soon as it is no longer needed?

☐ 4. Are locked containers for the disposal of classified information in document form conveniently located throughout the building?

☐ 5. Are these containers emptied frequently?

☐ 6. Have the destruction methods used for classified information in all forms been reviewed? Do they ensure that the information is completely destroyed and that it cannot be reconstructed in whole or in part?

Summary

The overview of the controls and procedures necessary to protect and destroy information discussed here are basic and require only common sense to implement. However, many companies do not have these controls and procedures in place; where they are in place, they often are not being followed.

Consistency is the key to information security. Security controls and procedures must be consistent with the value of the information being protected. Overprotection hampers efficiency, diverts security resources from more valuable information, and undermines the creditability of the entire program. Underprotection causes information-security exposures, leaving valuable information vulnerable.

All the areas discussed in this chapter are important to information security, and an information-security review should include all of them. Information security is the type of area where the lack of a single control, no matter how insignificant it may seem in the total information-security plan, could lead to a serious information-security exposure.

The ideas and checklists presented here can be tailored to meet a company's specific needs. The resultant checklist, however, must ensure that the auditor will not overlook any of the areas discussed when he or she conducts a review.

5

Protection in a Data Processing Environment

Business and government are vitally concerned with the vulnerability of information to loss while it is in a computer center. The National Bureau of Standards has the special responsibility of improving the controls and effectiveness of computer utilization in the federal sector while performing research and development activities whose results are available to the private and academic sectors.

The Institute of Internal Auditors, Inc., has recognized the need for controls in a computer environment and has undertaken the task of defining exposures, controls, and audit techniques. A new group of professionals, the EDP Auditors Association, was formed to deal with the phenomena of EDP audit and control. Respected associations like the Canadian Institute of Chartered Accountants and the EDP Auditors Association have also been pioneering the way in defining audit and control practices in the DP environment. The efforts of all these groups are broader than preventing unauthorized access to information. While it is generally recognized that accidental errors and omissions pose the most serious threat, these groups have recognized that a serious exposure to loss of information also exists in a DP environment. They have recommended various audit controls and techniques.

Today, the computer center creates, distributes, and maintains most of an organization's information. Advanced technology processes large quantities of information economically and efficiently. New hardware like graphic terminals can now process information such as design specifications. During the time the computer is processing such information as financial plans, new product designs, research and development activities, customer lists, and personnel information, this information is out of the control of the owner.

State of the Practice

Computer technology, including hardware and software, has advanced rapidly because of the need to create faster and more efficient methods and media for handling data. Data-security technology has made some effort to keep pace through developing new techniques and products. Encryption, if employed properly, provides better security than is possible in a nonautomated environment; and today's data processing vendors offer a veritable host of security tools. However, management seems more preoccupied with installing new and larger-capacity equipment and software programs to handle the ever-increasing amount of information that must be processed than with information security. Management procrastinates. It plans to implement an effective information-security plan as soon as the data processing environment is stabilized.

Unfortunately, data processing is a dynamic field with new and dramatic inventions being introduced almost daily, and the continuing advances in technology mean the DP environment is not going to stabilize in the near future. Management can no longer wait until later to implement an effective information-security program. It must use available tools and techniques now.

The National Bureau of Standards' recent, special publication *Audit and Evaluation of Computer Security* (No. 500-19) summarizes the state of the practice:

> The working group was extremely critical of the state of the practice in data processing. Much of what appears to be audit or security problems is, in reality, the institutionalism of bad practice . . . . It is ironic that a technology whose success depended on its ability to get its users to accept change is now threatened by the reluctance of its practitioners to accept change.[15]

The tremendous need to process increasing volumes of information brought about the growth of data processing; data processing, in turn, has brought about the rise of the data processing profession, the largest new profession of recent times. The profession's newness and the fact that it is generally measured on quantity and schedules rather than controls and quality greatly contribute to the state of the practice today.

Auditors as Catalysts

The Institute of Internal Auditors, Inc., has concluded:

> Internal auditors are faced with the task of investigating an environment in which most of them have only limited experience, knowledge, and tools.[16]

---

[15] U.S. Department of Commerce, National Bureau of Standards, *Audit and Evaluation of Computer Security — Publication 500-19* (Washington, D.C.: U.S. Government Printing Office), p. 37.

[16] *Systems Auditability and Control*, Vol. 3, Executive Report (Altamonte Springs, FL: The Institute of Internal Auditors, Inc., 1977), p. 6.

The fact that the auditing profession has not been involved in data processing controls has contributed significantly to the poor state of the practice in data processing security. Today, however, through the efforts of The Institute of Internal Auditors, Inc., the American Institute of Certified Public Accountants, and the EDP Auditors Association, and other professional groups, data processing auditors have come into being. They, along with certified public accountants, CPA specialists, and the internal audit profession itself must now catalyze management to move with haste to improve data processing security as a whole and information security in a data processing environment in specific.

Basic Administrative Controls Important in DP Environment

The computer center and related data processing functions are much like other information-service functions. The main differences are that the information in a computer center is stored on different types of media (tapes and disks) and that access to it is available by running a program or using a terminal. The objectives of information security in both functions are, however, the same. As a result, the information-security precautions required in a data processing environment are no different from those required in other information-service functions. This is not to say that the sophisticated security techniques which can be designed into the hardware and software of computing systems are not important. They are; but "safes and vaults for removable storage media and paper shredding devices for sensitive listings and reports are an integral part of any comprehensive data-security program."[17]

Elaborate security measures designed into the hardware or software of a computer system will not prevent the computer operator from putting two-part paper on a printer and keeping one copy of classified output for himself or herself, nor will they keep an intruder out of the tape library. Basic administrative controls are an integral part of information security in a data processing environment, and they should be audited *now*.

Risk Management/Selective Information Identification

Risk management and selective information identification and protection are viable concepts in the data processing environment. If not managed properly, the costs associated with information security can be prohibitive in terms of human resources, dollar expenditures, and degradation of data processing services. Identifying the risks and applying the information-security resource where it will

---

[17] Harry Katzan, Jr., *Computer Data Security* (New York: Van Nostrand Reinhold Company, 1973), p. 4.

produce the greatest benefits are important in a data processing environment.

A quantitative risk analysis should ensure that:

Objectives of the security program are directly related to the missions of the agency.

Those charged with selecting specific security measures have quantitative guidance on the amount of resources it is reasonable to expend on each security measure.

Long-range planners have guidance in applying security considerations to such things as site selection, building design, hardware configurations and procurements, software systems, and internal controls.

An explicit security policy can be generated which identifies what is to be protected, which threats are significant, and who shall be responsible for executing, reviewing, and reporting the security program.[18]

For these reasons, DP facility management should begin development of the security program with a risk analysis.

Scope of Information Security in a DP Environment

A basic knowledge of the data processing environment and a specific knowledge of the security practices and procedures necessary in that environment are prerequisites for conducting an information-security audit encompassing more than fundamental, administrative controls. For information on these subjects, the reader can refer to the following recent publications:

An Analysis of Computer Security Safeguards for Detecting and Preventing Intentional Computer Misuse, National Bureau of Standards Publication 500-25, January 1978. This report describes 132 safeguards for detection and 56 for prevention. It identifies those data processing security techniques that are specific to unauthorized disclosure of information.

Computer Control and Audit, The Institute of Internal Auditors, Inc., 1978. Three certified public accountants define the necessary controls in a data processing environment.

Computer Controls Guidelines and *Computer Audit Guidelines,* The Canadian Institute of Chartered Accountants, 1970, 1975. These two volumes define the controls necessary in a computer environment. Extensive checklists for the auditor are included.

---

[18] U.S. Department of Commerce, National Bureau of Standards, *Federal Information Processing Standards — Publication No. 31* (Washington, D.C.: U.S. Government Printing Office, 1974), p. 9.

Computer Data Security, Harry Katzan, Van Nostrand Reinhold, 1973. Three of the chapters present the basics of computers as they relate to data security.

Security, Accuracy, and Privacy in Computer Systems, James Martin, Prentice-Hall, 1973. An extensive compilation of known techniques on these subjects provides practical solutions to security problems.

Systems Auditability and Control, The Institute of Internal Auditors, Inc., 1977. These three research reports, funded by IBM for $500,000, define the state of the art of auditing in the data processing environment and provide suggestions for implementing controls.

Data processing security is a broad subject encompassing a wide range of controls; information security is only one subset of data processing security. Therefore, these books, like most others on the subject, encompass areas other than information security.

This chapter reviews, outlines, and consolidates those data processing security exposures that relate to information security and discusses possible controls. A company should be able to tailor its own information-security checklists and conduct an information-security review from the discussion and checklists presented here. The references cited above will also help in developing an audit program. The readers should refer to the checklists in proceeding through this discussion of control areas:

- organizational data processing controls
- user/owner responsibilities
- computer operations
- bulk transmission
- remote computing
- new system design, development, testing, and implementation
- auditability
- cryptography

Companies not having qualified EDP auditors should have a qualified data processing professional from another computer installation or staff function or a consultant work with the internal auditor to conduct this part of the information-security review.

Data Processing Organization

For purposes of information security, maintaining the proper separation of duties within data processing functions is as important as maintaining the proper separation of duties within a payroll operation for protection against fraud. The organizational structure and corresponding controls can have a significant impact on information security.

Creating data, writing programs, maintaining tape and disk libraries, operating the computer, scheduling workload, and servicing the user are some of the more important functions performed under the broad heading of data processing. The organization of these functions and the corresponding controls can either help or hinder information security. For example, a librarian has access to many volumes of classified information but is unable to copy it if not allowed to operate the computer. Vice versa, classified data should not be given to the computer operator unless it is for a specific, authorized purpose.

Organizational structure should ensure that neither a single department nor an individual can create an information-security exposure. Maintaining a proper separation of duties requiring controlled interaction between departments and individuals can prevent or promptly detect attempts to breach information security. This means separating the duties of the user who creates the data and authorizes its processing, the programmer, the data processing control group, the librarian, and the computer operator, among others. Written job descriptions for each of these functions should include responsibilities for information security.

Figure 2 shows a model for a large data processing organization.

Any review of information security in a data processing environment requires an analysis of the organizational structure and job descriptions to ensure that a separation of duties is maintained. Auditors should follow individual jobs from start to finish to ensure that no information-security exposures exist because of inadequate separation of duties. They should also question key personnel about their information-security responsibilities.

Information-Security Representatives

Figure 2 shows that all key areas of data processing should have information-security representatives. These representatives must not only understand the organization's information-security requirements but ensure their implementation. They would report to, and perform a staff role for, data processing management; however, they should also have a dotted-line relationship to the site's information-security function. Security representatives would be responsible for interfacing between the data processing function and the information-security function; they would also play an important role in communicating with users. Need will determine the number of information-security representatives, where they report, and how active a role they should play in each data processing organization's information-security plan.

Line Organizational Controls

"Computer Operations" in this chapter discusses two other organizational control techniques, the data processing group and the cleared-operator concept. The point to remember is organizational controls. These organizational controls represent line rather than staff

Figure 2
Data Processing Organization Model

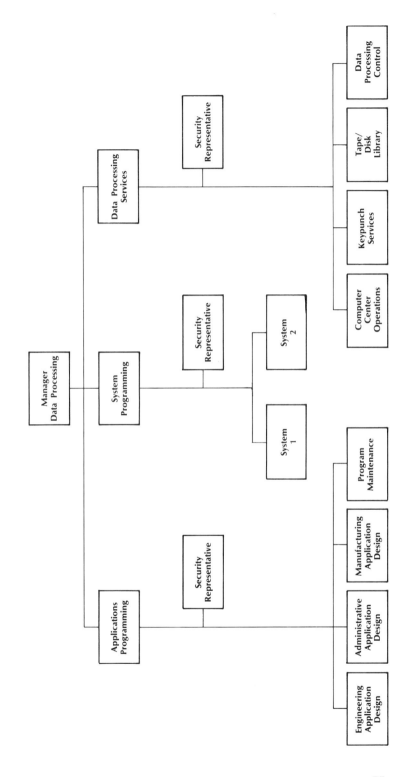

functions, but the important point is that organizational controls can greatly enhance information security.

Personnel Practices
Controls in the following personnel areas are equally applicable in a data processing environment.
- hiring practices
- certified acknowledgment-of-conduct guidelines
- positive employee's awareness and information-security education
- job rotation
- employee-exit interviews

Checklist 12
DP Organizational Controls

☐ 1. Is the organization structured so that a separation of duties is maintained?

☐ 2. Has a data processing control group been established to interface between users, programmers, and the computer room?

☐ 3. Have security representatives been appointed for vital functions within the organization?

☐ 4. Do written operating procedures include data processing information-security plans that have been approved by the security department?

☐ 5. Are data processing employees aware of their responsibilities for security? Have educational information-security classes been held?

☐ 6. Are employees and management in the user and data processing functions aware of who the data processing security representative is? Do they know how effective that representative has been?

☐ 7. Does the information-security representative play a key role during new system design?

☐ 8. Is the DP security representative involved in the planning for DP service, equipment, and facilities?

☐ 9. Have the following personnel practices been reviewed in relation to the DP function:
  - hiring practices
  - certified acknowledgment-of-conduct guidelines
  - job rotation
  - positive employee's awareness and information-security education
  - employee-exit interviews

User/Owner Responsibilities
Many organizations today have a "leave-it-to-the-data-processing-organization" syndrome. Users or owners of the data

relinquish all responsibility for, and sometimes even knowledge of, the data's existence as soon as they place it in the hands of the data processing organization. Auditors often make the mistake of confining their data processing security reviews to the data processing organization and not reviewing the owners' or users' responsibilities. The responsibility for protecting information is not solely that of the data processing organization. That organization is responsible for providing information-security tools and techniques and applying this protection consistent with the classification of the data and the instructions of the users/owners.

Users/owners of the data actually have the primary responsibility for the safekeeping of data. They should understand the various levels of security that can be afforded in the data processing environment, determine whether adequate security can be provided prior to putting the information in that environment, and communicate the specific data processing security requirements to the data processing function.

The "leave-it-to-data-processing" syndrome is analagous to a parent putting a child on a bus and sending him or her away to camp for the summer as a result of reading an ad in a newspaper. The parent has made no investigation into the reputation of the organization sponsoring the camp, has not seen the camp's location, and has not even communicated the special health needs of the child to the camp's staff.

The data processing organization, like the camp's staff, is a custodian and can only apply the information-security protection available as directed by the owners/users. The owners/users must determine whether the information-security protection available is adequate and is properly applied. Any review of data processing security that does not encompass the user's responsibilities and involvement will be incomplete.

Checklist 13
User/Owner Responsibilities in a Data Processing Environment

☐ 1. Has the user/owner selectively identified the sensitive data?
☐ 2. Does the user/owner understand the risks and exposures to loss of information that exist in the DP environment?
☐ 3. Does the user/owner understand the various protection facilities available (encryption, security control systems, password protection)?
☐ 4. Did the user/owner make a conscious decision that protection was adequate prior to placing the information in a DP environment?
☐ 5. Has the user/owner communicated the security needs of the information to the data processing function?
☐ 6. Does the user/owner effectively review and take action on reports of unauthorized access attempts to the information?

□ 7. Has the user/owner requested data processing reports showing who accessed sensitive data and when?

□ 8. Is there evidence that management reviews these reports?

□ 9. Has the user/owner restricted the authorized access list to the fewest-possible number of employees?

□ 10. Have key users (new product design, forecasting, financial planning) fulfilled their information-security responsibilities?

Computer Room Operations

The procedures controlling activities within the computer room play an important role in providing information security in a data processing environment. Common sense plays an equally important role. The following example illustrates the latter point.

In a large, multinational corporation, two men from the controller's office always witness the quarterly printing of the corporate financial statements. They take special care to see that no one in the computer room manages to see the figures. When the printing is finished, the two men carefully cut the output from the printer and, still taking precautions that no one see the statements, carry them out of the computer room. The fact that the print tape, with all the data intact, is still mounted on the drive is a source of considerable amusement to the computer operators.[19]

Obviously, these men did not use common sense in protecting the information, and the computer center did not install commonsense precautions to protect and limit access to tapes containing sensitive information.

Computer center personnel do not have a need to know; but, because of the nature of their jobs, they do require access to sensitive information. The design of computer-room procedures should limit access to sensitive information whenever possible, provide for authorization of access, maintain records of access, and control access by maintaining a proper separation of duties.

The majority of the security precautions to be discussed in this section apply to a local, batch-processing environment rather than a remote-processing environment. Security considerations applying to the use of terminal devices to access the computer are discussed later in this chapter.

Data Processing Control Groups

The use of a data processing control group, as shown in Figure 2, can strengthen organizational controls and help eliminate separation of duty problems. "They provide a service to users and exercise control for management."[20] A control group could be

---

[19] Brandt R. Allen, "Computer Security," Data Management, January 1972, p. 20.

[20] IBM Corporation, The Considerations of Physical Security in a Computer Environment, form number 6520-2700-0 (White Plains, New York: IBM Corporation), p. 13.

responsible for such things as verifying the proper authorization of a user's request, scheduling jobs, setting up normally scheduled jobs, approving or ensuring proper approval is obtained for reruns and special requests, maintaining records of when sensitive jobs are run and by whom, and ensuring that processed output is distributed to authorized employees only.

Data processing control groups serve as a liaison for most functions concerned with data processing and are an important part of the organizational controls. They should be independent within the data processing organization and not report to either operations, programming, or user management. It is also suggested that "the control area be outside the computer room but adjacent to it."[21]

A data processing control group can effectively implement some of the procedures required for controlling access to both the computer center and sensitive data.

Computer Center Access Control

The computer center should be housed within an island of security, even if it is for the physical protection of the equipment rather than for information-security reasons. A computer center with restricted access is called a "closed shop." Although the need for restricted access should be obvious, many computer centers are still "open shops." Actually, the only people who need unlimited access to the computer center are those who work directly in it.

> This freedom of access can create a significant security problem as well as result in lowered productivity of the facility. Normal access should be given only to the people who regularly work in the area. Anyone else should be given access on a controlled basis.[22]

Computer centers should have only one authorized entrance; all other doors should be locked, have alarms and be used only as emergency exits. A single entrance will not generally cause inconvenience because most computer centers are not very large. Access can be permitted through the use of keys or magnetic badges. Magnetic badges are preferable because they are more difficult to duplicate and make easier the identification of authorized personnel.

Computerized systems can also control access. One of these systems operates the same as the 24-hour bank teller. An employee inserts a card into a slot and enters a numerical security code known only by him or her. The card must still be on the active file, and the numerical code must be correct to unlock the door. Such

---

[21] *Ibid.*, p. 22.

[22] IBM Corporation, *Forty-two Suggestions for Improving Security in Data Processing Operations*, form number 6520-2169 (White Plains, New York: IBM Corporation), p. 3.

a system has several advantages. Lost cards can be removed from the active file, and a record is maintained of all movement. Such a system can also be used to control access to the building and other islands of security.

Only management should authorize access, no matter which access method is used. Also, unless the entrance is manned, tailgating will still exist. Locating the data processing control group by the computer center entrance will overcome this problem. The group can monitor access or use a "person-trap" entrance. Here, the employee gains entrance through the first door with a key or badge but cannot enter the second door unless a person monitoring a closed-circuit television screen recognizes him or her.

Most security requirements pertaining to authorized access to the security of a computer center are the same as those necessary for any other island of security. A complete list is presented again in Checklist 13. Most companies are proud of their computer centers and like to show them off to outsiders who may be on a tour of the building. Obvious reasons make this an inadvisable practice. Banks do not give tours of their vaults; why should a company conduct a tour through one of its most sensitive and vital areas?

Data-Access Control

Preventing unauthorized access to data requires controls to ensure that:

1. Only authorized employees are allowed in the computer room (already discussed in the previous section).
2. Only authorized users can request data processing services.
3. Only authorized users can access classified files, and a record of access is maintained.
4. Classified computer output is distributed to authorized recipients.
5. Classified information on data files is destroyed when no longer necessary.

Requiring that each job submitted to the computer center be accompanied by a job request form signed by appropriate management can prevent unauthorized users from obtaining data processing services. The kind of management approval required depends on the type of service being requested and whether the data being accessed is classified or unclassified.

Normally scheduled jobs like payroll and accounts payable are easier to control because the data processing control group knows from experience who is authorized to submit them. Blanket authorization can be used to allow the running of normally scheduled jobs. For example, "Tom Jones is authorized to request the running of the payroll program every Friday." Signed, Mr. Payroll Manager.

Any data processing service that is not part of the normal routine and requires access to classified data requires specific approval. This includes deviations in the running of normally scheduled jobs, modifying sensitive programs, and copying data files.

All job request forms should include at a minimum the requestor's name, what data is going to be accessed, and the classification of the output. The control clerk or librarian, by comparing this information with a listing of who has authorized access, can ensure that access is authorized prior to submitting the request and files to the computer operator.

This technique controls access to privately owned, removable storage volumes such as the tapes and disks normally used in a batch-processing environment. However, if permanently mounted storage devices such as drums or disks are used for public storage (many users' data reside on the same file), the manual security controls can be augmented by a system-security technique. The system compares an identification code provided by the user on the job card with an authorization table maintained within the system. If the identification code cannot be found in the authorization table, the job is terminated. One problem with this method is that job decks used to initiate computer processing contain the identifying information necessary for access to sensitive files and are handled by the user, the control group, and the operator. Whether the identifying information is easily readable, it is a simple process to duplicate the job deck. Therefore, any job deck used to access sensitive files should be classified the same as the information it allows access to, and it should also be protected in a manner consistent with its classification.

A record of all sensitive jobs submitted to the computer room should be maintained. It should include when the job was submitted, who submitted it, what machine was used to process it, and the final disposition of the job and its output. The control group should keep sensitive computer output in a secure environment until it can be distributed to an authorized recipient.

Often magnetic tapes or direct-access devices are used for temporary storage of sensitive information. It is not sufficient to reuse these volumes again and assume that the original data has been overwritten and thus destroyed. "Experiments have been performed to demonstrate that it is possible to recover information which has been overwritten by other information."[23] There are hardware features available which can completely erase the contents of tapes or disks.

The general security precautions for access control to information in a computer room as discussed here are not so important to the internal auditor as the fact that his or her company is meeting the objectives presented.

---

[23] Dennis Van Tassel, *Computer Security Management* (Englewood Cliffs, New Jersey: Prentice-Hall, Inc., 1972), pp. 153-154.

Cleared Operators

Another organizational method of limiting the number of people who have access to sensitive information within a computer room is by assigning certain operators to handle sensitive jobs. Through the use of cleared operators, access to sensitive programs and data can be limited. A cleared operator would have the responsibility for maintaining the confidentiality of the job and all data related to it while it is in the computer room. One cleared operator could process an entire job from the time it is read into the system until the tapes are returned to the library and the output is given to the control group. Cleared operators could also be assigned various tasks within the computer room.

The cleared-operator concept can strengthen the audit trail of those having access to sensitive data. The control group or the tape librarian could actually record the fact that John Doe processed the customer-list program or had access to the customer files. Operators are less likely to attempt a breach of information security if the loss of information can be traced back to them, and they are more likely to take extra steps in safeguarding the information if they have been specifically given this responsibility.

Media Libraries

The greatest accumulation of sensitive information within a company resides on tapes and disks, referred to as "files." The security precautions taken to protect these files are vital to any information-security program.

All files should be stored within a library, assuming that the security precautions taken within the library are adequate. Storage of files in a user's, or programmer's area is unacceptable because they lose the accountability and protection the library affords.

The library should be a separate island of security within the computer center. Only the librarians should have access to it. Users, programmers, and computer operators have no need to access the library.

All files should be serially controlled. Adequate records must be maintained of to whom a file is allocated and who is authorized to access it. Files containing sensitive information should be allocated to the management of the using function, and only management should be authorized to access them. It is particularly helpful for control purposes to allocate series of files to a particular category, a particular user, or both. For example, files in the series 1XXXX contain sensitive information; and 12XXX volumes are allocated to the payroll department.

All volumes should have external labelling of their contents and classification. The color of the label can designate the sensitivity of the data. "For instance, highly classified data would reside on red tapes, data which only a few people can access would reside on blue tapes, and all other data would reside on grey tapes."[24]

The user should indicate the classification of a volume when he or she requests it, and the records should indicate either the classification of the tape or the fact that it is unclassified. In this way, it can be determined that a conscious decision was made to declare a volume unclassified and that the classification process was not just overlooked.

Inventories of all volumes should be taken periodically, and the user should be notified if a volume is not located. The frequency of the inventories depends on the classification of the data. Top-priority files should be inventoried weekly; secret files, quarterly; and all other files, semiannually. It is also advisable to periodically (semiannually) send user managements a list of the files allocated to them, the names of those they have authorized to access them, and the data classification. Periodic recertification accomplishes the following objectives:
- user management verification of classification
- accuracy of the access list to classified files
- management reminder of responsibility

In this way, data which is no longer needed can be destroyed; and the authorized access list and classification of data can be kept current.

Utility Control

Certain data processing utilities are necessary to provide the computer operations department the ability to maintain the operating systems. Though they provide capabilities to bypass security controls and execute data files or programs, they serve a valid business need and are a necessary evil. Programs which can bypass information protection or "zap" fixes to programs or data should be identified. Their use should be restricted to one or two system programmers on system programs; unauthorized use can have a severe negative impact on information security. There is generally no business need other than convenience to use most of these types of programs on applications or data. When such use becomes absolutely necessary, specific management authorization should be required.

Checklist 14
Computer Operations

☐ 1. Are there documented security procedures for computer operations?

☐ 2. Do these procedures take into account the fact that computer center personnel do not have a need to know but do require access?

---

[24] Op. cit., Considerations of Physical Security, p. 12.

☐ 3. Has a data processing control group been established to strengthen security controls?

☐ 4. Has the effectiveness of the control group's efforts been reviewed?

☐ 5. Is the computer center housed within an island of security?

☐ 6. Is access restricted at all times to personnel authorized by management?

☐ 7. Is a current list of authorized personnel maintained by management? Does management keep the number of authorized personnel to an absolute minimum? Is access by programmers and users on an exception basis controlled?

☐ 8. Have visitor control procedures been established? Do they require escorting? Do they sign in and out? Do they include noncompany employees (vendors) as well as employees whose primary work station is outside the computer room?

☐ 9. Are electronic alarms or other devices which detect movement by either sound or light rays used during periods when no one should be in the area?

☐ 10. Are these alarms or devices hooked up to the guards' central control station?

☐ 11. Are they tested?

☐ 12. Is closed-circuit television surveillance of the computer room necessary? Is it used?

☐ 13. Are procedures for cleaning the computer installation reviewed? Are cleaners escorted?

☐ 14. Have admittance procedures been reviewed? If badges are used, are the badges color-coded to designate authorized access to the computer room? Are they worn at all times by computer center employees?

☐ 15. If badges are issued by a central group like the guard force, is a list of people possessing these badges periodically sent to computer center management for review?

☐ 16. Do procedures ensure the return of a badge if an employee leaves the function or the company?

☐ 17. If access is gained through cipher locks, is the combination changed periodically? Is it changed automatically when an employee leaves the function?

☐ 18. If access is gained by keys, who has keys? Is there effective control of keys?

☐ 19. Are there adequate controls to ensure that only authorized users may request data processing services?

    • Does a request for data processing services require management approval?

    • Is particular attention given to controlling special requests (including copying data files, changing programs, and deviations in the running of normally scheduled jobs)?

☐ 20. Does the job request form include at a minimum the

requestor's name, files to be accessed, and classification of output?

☐ 21. Is access to sensitive data files adequately controlled?
  • If public storage is used, does the system have a security routine to verify authorization of access to sensitive files?
  • Have procedures for updating and maintaining the authorization tables been reviewed?
  • Is authorization of access granted only by management of the owning department? (This applies only if central control authorization tables are maintained. In some systems, each user controls security codes for his or her files.)
  • Are controls in place to ensure that unauthorized changes to the authorization tables cannot take place?
  • Is management of the owning departments periodically sent a list of who has been authorized access to their files for review?

☐ 22. Are job decks clearly stamped with their classification? Are the classifications equivalent to the data they access?

☐ 23. Are operators or data control center personnel denied access to program flowcharts, source decks, or source (program) listings? (They do not need this information, and denying them access to it prevents them from changing or running programs.)

☐ 24. Have cleared operators been specifically designated the responsibility of security for sensitive jobs while they are in the computer center? If not, how is access to sensitive programs, files, and output controlled in the computer room?

☐ 25. Are only authorized personnel in processing areas when sensitive jobs are run?

☐ 26. Is the console log used as an audit trail and to monitor the actions taken by the operator?
  • Does it record at a minimum all jobs entered to the system, any significant events, and all files accessed by a job?
  • Is it at least periodically reviewed by management?
  • Are there controls in place to prevent the operator from disposing of pages (prenumbered sheets or storing console activity on a tape or disk file to be periodically printed and reviewed by management)?

☐ 27. Is printed output clearly labelled with the classification of the information? (This is a function of the program which created the report.)

☐ 28. Is sensitive output kept secure until it is distributed?
  • Are recipients of output authorized by appropriate management?
  • If possible, is it signed for?

☐ 29. Are sensitive, removable storage devices (tapes and disks) returned to the library immediately after processing?

☐ 30. Is a log maintained of sensitive jobs submitted to the computer center? Does it provide an audit trail which includes when the job was submitted, by whom, the cleared operator it was given to for processing, when it was completed, and to whom the output was distributed?

☐ 31. Did tracing the flow of sensitive jobs through the computer room disclose any data security problem?

☐ 32. Is the library housed within a separate island of security adjacent to the computer center?

☐ 33. Is access to the library restricted to librarians? (Programmers, operators, and users do not need access.)

☐ 34. Are tapes and disks allocated to user management?

☐ 35. At the time of allocation, is user management required to indicate the classification of the data?

☐ 36. Are all tapes and disks labelled externally with their classification?

☐ 37. Is access to tapes and disks containing sensitive data controlled through written authorization from user management?

☐ 38. Are all tapes and disks serially controlled?

☐ 39. Are tapes and disks containing sensitive information segregated by their physical location in the library or by a separate series of numbers or both?

☐ 40. Is an inventory listing of tapes and disks maintained?

- serial number
- description of data
- classification
- user management it was allocated to
- authorized users

☐ 41. Is this list referred to when a user requests access to sensitive tapes or disks?

☐ 42. Is a physical inventory of all sensitive tapes and disks taken periodically?

☐ 43. Is follow-up action taken and user management notified when files are not located?

☐ 44. Do procedures ensure timely and adequate destruction of sensitive information stored on tapes and disks when it is no longer needed?

☐ 45. Does the library periodically supply user management with a list of tapes and disks allocated to them and the names of those who have authorized access?

☐ 46. Has operations management recognized the danger of un-authorized use of some powerful utilities?

☐ 47. Have they identified these utilities?

☐ 48. What controls have they put in place to restrict access to these utilities?

☐ 49. Is access restricted to one or two system programmers with an absolute need?

66

☐ 50. Is use restricted to system programs and not application programs or data?

☐ 51. Is there a log of all use of these utilities?

☐ 52. Has the log to ensure only system programs have been accessed by these utilities except in specially approved instances been reviewed?

Bulk Data Transmission

Data files can be transmitted between locations by physical transfer or by electronic means. In either case, the proprietor of the data (user management) should authorize the transmission in writing.

If data files are physically transferred, the transfer should be accomplished between the librarians at the two locations through preestablished procedures. The procedures should include communicating the classification of the data being transferred and the name of the person authorized to access it at the receiving location. The librarian at the receiving location can then verify the identity of that person, and exposure to an unauthorized recipient is minimized. The method of shipment must be consistent with the classification of the data, and receipt acknowledgment should be required.

The transmission of data by electronic means requires similar control procedures. The proprietor must submit written authorization. The sending location should identify the receiving location prior to transmission, communicate the classification, and indicate the authorized recipient. The receiving location should acknowledge receipt and secure the data in the library. Since the transmission of data by electronic means is subject to wire tapping, it may require encoding. The subject of cryptography in a data processing environment is discussed later in this chapter.

Bulk transmission of data is an area requiring detailed organization-wide procedures to ensure consistent information-security practices.

Checklist 15:
Bulk Data Transmission

☐ 1. Are both the electronic and physical transfers of bulk data adequately controlled?

☐ 2. Is user management required to submit written authorization to have sensitive files transmitted?

☐ 3. Does physical transfer of sensitive files take place only between libraries?

☐ 4. Does the method of sending sensitive files provide protection consistent with the classification of the data?

☐ 5. When sending sensitive data electronically, does the location:
- identify the receiving location prior to transmission?
- communicate the classification of the data and name the authorized recipient?

- document the authorizing individual, time of transmittal, name of receiving-location individual, and classification?
☐ 6. When receiving sensitive data transmitted electronically, does the location document time of receipt, transmitting-location individual, classification, and authorized recipients?
☐ 7. Is the data delivered directly to the librarian?
☐ 8. Whether sensitive data is transferred physically or electronically, is receipt acknowledged?
☐ 9. Are the location's practices in compliance with the organization's requirements?
☐ 10. Are the practices for mailing and electronically transmitting bulk data observed?
☐ 11. Do the procedures followed in shipping and storing of vital information for backup purposes in case of an emergency provide adequate security?
☐ 12. Is the user requested to specify whether data to be transmitted should be encrypted?

Remote Computing

Remote computing involves the use of any input or output device located outside the computer room to access the computer. It incorporates terminals and remote job-processing stations that have input and output devices to communicate with the main computer installation.

Unlike batch processing which takes place within the computer center, remote computing requires information to be stored on public storage devices. Since a remote-computing system can have upward of 1,000 users, it would be impractical to load or unload storage devices as needed. With so many users having access to large data banks of information, new security exposures are created. Harry Katzan, Jr., describes these exposures as follows:

> First, the computer operator is usually not involved in the situation to identify a job or a request for data.
> Second, an unauthorized person can easily masquerade as an authorized person.
> Third, data communications facilities are frequently used in remote access, and the user must be concerned with the security of both the terminal device and the communications facilities.[25]

Katzan also states: "This type of security problem is usually solved by providing terminal protection, identifying the terminal, identifying the user, and providing different levels of protection."[26]

---

[25] Op. cit., Katzan, p. 105.

[26] Ibid.

Levels of Protection

In a remote-computing environment, the method of authenticating users and determining what information they are authorized to access is accomplished at three levels:

- terminal identification
- user identification
- resource authorization

The value and exposure to loss of the data being secured determines the level of protection to be applied.

Terminal Identification

Terminal identification is the process of ensuring that only authorized terminals can access the computer system or data. When terminals are located within the same building as the computer, private communication lines can be used to connect the terminal and the computer. In this situation, only the terminals that have been "hard wired" to the computer can gain access.

When common carrier (telephone and telegraph) communication lines are used, the computer system must be able to identify the terminal requesting access. Terminal identification can be accomplished by programming the computer to respond only to terminals at a given address. The address would be part of the terminal message, and the computer would refer to a list of authorized terminal addresses before responding.

Terminal identification can also be accomplished through the use of a unique, tamper-free identification code.

User Identification

The security of many systems today depends primarily on the identification of the authorized user. Identification can be made through the use of a security code, generally referred to as a password. A table of authorized users and their passwords is maintained within the system. When users sign on, they must enter their names or employees' serial numbers and passwords issued to them. The system verifies that the particular password and the name are related and that the user is authorized before allowing him or her to proceed. The disadvantage of this technique is that passwords can be accidentally exposed to others. There are complex variations to the simple password technique described here, but they are both tedious and time-consuming.

A key or badge inserted into the terminal provides another method of user identification. It can be used together with passwords or separately. The advantage of this technique is that a lost key or badge would be noticed immediately and that corrective action could be taken, whereas a password could be compromised and go unnoticed.

Experiments with other methods of user identification are being carried on but are not yet commercially available.

Resource Authorization
After an individual has been verified as an authorized user, it must be determined what function, programs, or data he or she is authorized to access. Besides verifying the medium (badge, key, or password) used to sign on with, the system should have a table containing the user's authorization level to check. For example, prior to allowing access to new product design specifications, the system will compare the user's password with a table of passwords authorized to access the data.

Data files can also be protected by using "lock words," security codes applied at the data file level. Depending on the system, lock words will be supplied by the user and changed at his or her discretion; or they will be assigned and maintained by an individual who is responsible for the security of that system. The system will deny access to any resource if the user cannot respond with the correct lock word for that data.

Security Codes
The proper design and administration of security codes is vital to the security of information in a remote-computing environment. Five key elements ensure proper protection:
- uniqueness
- randomness
- change frequency
- disclosure prevention
- privileged codes

The controls function under either system design or administration because sometimes the required result can be achieved by the system; at other times, it can be accomplished through manual administration.

Security codes (passwords or lock words) should be unique to an individual or data set; multiple users or data sets dilute security. Sharing a password among several users defeats the primary purpose of being able to identify all transactions with a single user.

Users should not adopt security codes such as their initials, first names, or office numbers that are too easily guessed. Ideally, system-generated security codes using a random number table are best; however, many systems allow users to create their own security code. In this case, an administrative control must be implemented to ensure passwords are not easily figured out.

Passwords should be changed periodically so that, if compromised, the period of exposure is limited. Bimonthly is generally accepted as a reasonable period of change. The best methods of ensuring that passwords are changed at the times specified is to have the system generate the new passwords automatically or lock out users who did not change their security codes.

Designing the system so that the terminal will not print or display the characters when the security code is being entered or so that the security code will be written over by other characters prevents disclosure of a security code as it is entered into the terminal. It is the responsibility of the user to protect the password by destroying anything the password is printed on and ensuring that no one else is in the area when the password is presented on the terminal.

A privileged security code is generally assigned to the system administrator to allow maintenance of the system. Privileged security codes are also used to authorize new users to the system, generate new security codes, and determine what a security code was in the event one gets lost. Limiting privileged security codes to the fewest possible number of people is crucial to the security of the system.

Terminal Protection

Terminal protection requires housing the terminal within an island of security to prevent unauthorized use. At remote locations where many terminals are used, housing all terminals within a single island of security will control access. If this is not feasible, minimum protection can be afforded by locking the terminal when it is not in use. If the terminal is not lockable with a key, a locking mechanism can be fabricated for the power-on-and-off switch or a lock can be placed on the data phone.

The posting of system phone numbers, security codes, and other instructions should be strictly prohibited in the terminal or remote job-entry area. Further, all system output should be removed or locked up when the terminal work has been completed.

Auditability

Every remote-computing system should provide records of authorized and unauthorized activities to management. First, the very existence of such records serves as a deterrent to unauthorized access attempts. Second, in the event of an unauthorized disclosure of proprietary information, audit trails as to who accessed the information and when are invaluable in determining how the incident occurred.

Reporting unauthorized access attempts to data prevents a perpetrator from continually trying different methods to access data until success is achieved. Knowledge that a report of unauthorized access attempts exists is also an excellent deterrent.

The subject of auditability as it relates to all data processing resources is covered later in this chapter.

Telecommunications Facilities

It is possible to tap data transmission lines to obtain data just as phone lines can be tapped to hear conversations. In many cases, it does not involve extraordinary cost. Terminal telephone closets and switching rooms exist in most locations; and the numbers of dataphones are, like all other phone numbers, clearly displayed. It is not difficult to place two alligator clips on the terminals for a data phone and record the transmission of data. All telecommunication facilities must be adequately secured.

System Administration

In a remote-computing environment, the system administration group typically ensures information security by:
- authorizing new users
- assigning security codes
- changing security codes
- distributing unauthorized access reports
- distributing authorized access reports
- deleting users from system
- maintaining the general system

The system administration group generally possesses a privileged security code. Controls must be in place to ensure the group performs its duties in keeping with information security.

Checklist 16:
Remote Computing

☐ 1. Does use of the system require written management authorization? Compare the list of users with written authorizations on file.

☐ 2. Does the remote-computing system provide for terminal identification to ensure only authorized terminals can access system resources? This is particularly important when common carriers (telephone and telegraph lines) are used.

☐ 3. Is there a method such as a password, key, or badge to identify that a user is authorized?

☐ 4. Is access control to date on the system administered at the right level to ensure that only employees with an authorized need to know have access to proprietary information?

☐ 5. Are security codes (passwords or lock words) controlled?
- Are they unique to a data set or individual? (shared security codes dilute accountability and weaken security.)
- Are they selected randomly? (Convenient and easily guessed passwords should not be allowed.)
- Are security codes changed frequently? (For secret data, the frequency of change should not exceed two months. The

auditor should review the distribution procedure for new codes.)

- Are precautions taken to prevent the compromise of passwords on printed or display output?
- Who has privileged codes? Is their use limited to the fewest-possible number of employees, and is it controlled?

☐ 6. Is the terminal area secure?
- Is classified information destroyed or locked up?
- Is access to the area or terminal restricted? For terminal rooms or remote job-entry stations, refer to the island-of-security checklist, number five.)
- Are passwords, system phone numbers, or user's manuals left in the area?

☐ 7. Does the remote-computing facility provide the function of auditability so that it can be determined who had access to information?

☐ 8. Does the user-management community review reports of authorized and unauthorized access attempts to ensure that the system is being used as intended and that unauthorized access has not occurred?

☐ 9. Are telecommunication facilities (phone closets) secure?

☐ 10. Does the system provide the capability to encrypt information?

☐ 11. Is this capability being used?

☐ 12. Review the duties being performed by the system administration function.
- Does this function coordinate the information-security activities of the users?
- Have they provided adequate information-security knowledge?
- Is an information-security bulletin published?
- Do users understand the security weaknesses inherent in the system?
- Is adequate control over authorization tables maintained? When employees leave the function, is their access terminated immediately?

☐ 13. Review the responsibilities of the user.
- Are secure terminal areas maintained?
- Are passwords changed frequently if user controlled?
- Do users follow established procedures?
- Do they remain at the terminal during printouts of sensitive data?
- Have they limited authorized access to the fewest-possible number of employees?

☐ 14. If media exist in the remote-processing facility, are they controlled in conjunction with Checklist 14?

☐ 15. Is the top-priority document control center involved in the creation of top-priority data?

New System Design, Development, Testing, and Implementation

The precautions taken during the design, development, testing, and implementation of a new system can either enhance data security or create significant exposures to loss of information. The role of the auditor in system design is currently being debated throughout the audit profession. Should auditors be directly involved in the design and development of new systems and provide the benefit of their control knowledge? Or once auditors participate in the design of the system, will they lose the objectivity required to conduct a postimplementation review? Both sides of the question have merit. Also, the characteristics of the organization greatly influence the auditor's role. For example, where new system design activity consists of one program a year, direct audit participation may be feasible. However, in an organization which has several thousand programmers working on new design, it may be impractical.

Determining the auditor's role in system design is dependent on many factors; however, one thing is extremely clear. The auditor does have a responsibility to ensure that the information systems designed are secure.

To fulfill this responsibility, the auditor may either participate directly in the system's design or he or she may audit the management process for system design. Both roles are effective; yet they are clearly different, as will be explained in the next two sections of this chapter. Audit organizations must determine for themselves which role or combination of roles is suitable for their particular environment.

Auditor Participation in System Design

An auditor's direct involvement in the design of a new system has a twofold benefit. First, being independent of the function being programmed, the auditor has no preconceived ideas. He or she wants mainly to ensure that adequate controls are designed into the system. This independent concern for controls serves as a strong check and balance, ensuring that other requirements of the system do not adversely effect the need for controls.

Second, the auditor brings a knowledge of controls that few other professionals have, and this knowledge can significantly strengthen the information-security controls in a system. Auditors' responsibilities in this capacity include directly participating in each phase of the review, reviewing all system documentation, and recommending controls. In some organizations, the audit function's nonconcurrence with a phase will prevent moving on to the next phase.

Auditor participation in system design, particularly where the security of highly sensitive information is involved, can result in a more secure system.

Auditing the Management Process for Design

When audit participation in new system design is not practical or when a supplemental audit procedure is needed, reviewing the management process for system design ensures a secure information system. This audit concentrates on the management controls for good design as contrasted to the internal controls necessary for a specific design in which the auditor is directly involved.

If the auditor does not participate in the detail design of the system, the independent role can be — and perhaps should be — fulfilled by the information-security department or a quality-assurance function within information systems or both.

An audit of the management process for system design would involve sampling recently completed and currently developing projects in various phases of the cycle and determining if certain controls, to be discussed in the following section, are installed. A simple overview of the auditor's role in system design and a management process for system design are presented. More detailed discussion of these subjects are available in *Systems Auditability and Control* (SAC project, three volumes) and *Computer Control and Audit,* both published by The Institute of Internal Auditors, Inc.

Management Process for System Design

In Figure 3, the management process to ensure the development of information-secure systems shows six phases of the development cycle. While the actual phases in the development cycle within a given organization may be named differently or include more or fewer phases, the phases described here relate to the logical functions that must be performed.

The six phases of the development cycle are general design, detail design, programming, test, implementation, and maintenance.

Phase 1, General Design, begins with the conception of an idea or need. During this phase, the need is defined in general terms; and the feasibility of the idea is studied. Sometimes Phase 1 is called the "feasibility phase."

Information-security exposures inherent in the new idea must be identified at this time, and the feasibility of providing adequate information security must be considered prior to proceeding with development. Phase 1 results in a document called "general design specifications." These general specifications should include a separate and comprehensive statement of information-security objectives.

After an idea is determined feasible from a functional, economic, technical, and information-security viewpoint, it proceeds to Phase 2, Detail Design. During Phase 2, the general idea is translated into detailed descriptions as to how the system will be

Figure 3
Management Process for Design

Key Elements	Phase 1 General Design	Phase 2 Detail Design	Phase 3 Programming	Phase 4 Test	Phase 5 Implementation	Phase 6 Maintenance
Documentation:						
General Design (Information-Security Objective)	X					
Detail Design (Information-Design Techniques)		X				
Test Plan				X		X
Test Results				X		X
User's Manual					X	X
Operations Manual					X	X
Systems Manual						
Phase Review	X	X	X	X	X	X
Functions Involved:						
Programming	X	X	X	X	X	X
User	X	X	X	X	X	X
Information Security	X	X	X	X	X	X
DP Operations	X	X	X	X	X	X
*Audit	X	X	X	X	X	X
Education:	—	—	—	—	X	X

* Audit involvement in the design process is dependent upon the organization's policy; however, any system processing highly proprietary data should be subject to comprehensive information-security review six months after implementation.

designed and how it will operate. The specifications produced are critical and should include a separate and comprehensive statement of information-security techniques. How the information-security objectives outlined in Phase 1 will be implemented is determined in this phase. Phase 2 is the most important of all the phases because the information-security tools and techniques are designed here. The remaining phases are incidental to implementing the information-security techniques and plans designed in this phase.

Phase 3 is where the actual coding to accomplish the design is performed. Documentation should include a test plan and documented test results that will demonstrate that the information-security controls defined in Phase 2 are working.

Phase 4 is where the coding is tested to determine if the objectives, techniques, and functions provided for in the design were accomplished.

Phase 5 is where the system is implemented and when conversion from the old system takes place. Documentation in this phase includes a complete systems manual, a user's manual, and an operations manual. The systems manual is generally a complete overview and description of the system in technical terms. The intended audience of system documentation is the programming function. The user's manual should clearly define the system and administrative controls for information security as well as the responsibilities for system-information security. The operations manual should define the operations functions's responsibility for information security.

In both Phase 4 and Phase 5, testing and implementation, additional controls are necessary to protect information. The system designers should not have uncontrolled access to highly proprietary data. They do not have a need to know; and their need to access must be restricted to a bare minimum. Generally, access to live data is not necessary during the testing phase; test data can be generated in place. In both of these phases, system-developer access should require user's and programmer management's approval.

During system design, the internal auditor has the responsibility of conducting a postimplementation review to ensure that information-security controls are operational and effective. A good rule of thumb as to when to conduct these reviews is six months after installation. This gives development and user management time to get the "bugs" out and fine tune the operation of the new system.

The audit staff should maintain a list of new development projects. All applications that will process highly proprietary information should be subject to a separate application review six months after installation.

Last, most applications are enhanced in Phase 6. Management controls in the maintenance phase ensure that (1) all system-related documentation is updated to reflect changes, (2) that enhancements do not affect established information-security controls, (3) that additional controls are designed when necessary, and (4) that information-security exposures are not created by allowing programmers uncontrolled access to live data.

Key Management Control Elements

The management process to be described has three key elements: documentation, review, and education.

Documentation

The program code, considered by many to be the most important part of new system documentation, may, in fact, be the least important. It is only incidental to a new system in that it instructs the computer. The system *documentation* is what defines the objectives, provides the foundation and framework to be used as the base of comparison in determining the function's need to be programmed, instructs how to use and operate the system, and communicates the system's functions.

Documentation serves four main information-security objectives by providing:
• a defined base of the information-security controls (including both system and administrative controls) requiring implementation
• users and operations management with instructions as to the information-security controls to be exercised
• the facility to enhance the system to improve information security or to prevent other enhancements from adversely affecting information security
• the ability to audit the system to determine the adequacy of information security

Documentation is written for many purposes other than information security; however, information security is a separate and explicit section of *all* documentation. The requirement to document information-security controls must be included in the management process for design. This requirement, which is subject to review by other people, is in itself an excellent control and deterrent to weak information security.

The auditor is an intended audience of documentation. If the auditor has difficulty in understanding a system's documentation, it can be reasonably assumed that the users of a system, who probably have less exposure to data processing, also will not understand it. Assessing the adequacy of a system's information security becomes impossible without good documentation.

Review

A comprehensive review of the system must be undertaken during each of the six phases to determine if the objectives of that phase have been accomplished before progressing to the next phase.

Information security should be an integral part of each of these phase reviews. Explicit documentation should demonstrate to the auditor that the phase reviews were conducted, that information security was addressed in a comprehensive manner, and that management from all appropriate functions was involved.

Management evidences its involvement by its formal sign-off indicating agreement or disagreement. From an information-security viewpoint, the management from the using, programming, information-security, and DP-operations functions should have to formally express concurrence or nonconcurrence in the results of each phase.

Education

Information security in a new system depends on the proper use of both the system and the administrative controls. Not using provided controls properly can only result in poor information security. Therefore, users and operators should be taught the proper use of these controls. Formal education classes should be held during the implementation phase, and refresher training should be scheduled periodically.

Key Elements of Information Security

Three key elements must be considered in designing a new system: access control, auditability, and encryption.

Access Control

The ability to control access to those with a need to know is the most important objective of designing a system with good information security. Control can be accomplished in various ways. For example, in an interactive system, access can be controlled by data set or by a category of data within a data set. In a financial planning system where multiple locations input data to headquarters, controlling access at the data-set level would not restrict access to those with a need to know. Giving *all* locations access to the data set would also give them access to the data of other locations for which they do not have a need to know. Access authorization to data in this case should be based on the location code rather than on the data-set level to prevent one location from accessing another location's data. Controls which limit access to data to the fewest-possible number of people with an authorized need to know are of paramount importance in new design.

Many systems provide *privileged* access to the administrator who must maintain the system. Such access may bring about the authorization of new users, the changing of passwords, and other necessary, but dangerous, functions. The design of privileged access techniques must be kept to a minimum, and a record identifying all privileged access must be designed into a new system.

Auditability

Auditability provides a comprehensive history of all authorized and unauthorized access. Being able to trace access to information to an individual controls and deters information-security incidents. Auditability is discussed more fully later in this chapter.

Encryption

For the purpose of information security, any system today that processes highly proprietary data must have the ability to encrypt data. Encryption is also discussed more fully later in this chapter.

Checklist 17
New System Design, Development, Test, and Implementation

□ 1. Is it required that all system documentation require a separate and explicit statement on information security?

□ 2. Review and comment on the adequacy of the following documentation in regard to information security:
  - general design specifications
  - detail design specifications
  - test plan
  - test results
  - user's manual
  - operator's manual
  - system manual

□ 3. Does the security plan include all manual controls and hardware of software security routines which will ensure that adequate protection is afforded to all the sensitive information which is created or used by the system including programs, data files, and output reports?

□ 4. Is a formal and well-documented review conducted after each phase?

□ 5. Do programming, user, DP operations, and information-security management sign off to indicate their concurrence or non-concurrence with the results of each phase?

□ 6. Are the key objectives of access control, auditability, and encryption adequately considered during design?

□ 7. Is access to live data effectively controlled during the test and implementation stage?

In this checklist, the steps listed apply equally to reviewing a postimplementation application of a single application or to auditing the management process for system design by sampling development projects.

Auditability

All attempts to access information must be explicitly recorded so that, in case of an information-security incident, it can be determined what people had authorized access to what information and when.

A number of logs can provide an audit trail and monitor threats to information security. The console log, normally available but seldom used, monitors all action taken by the computer operator. Console printouts generally record the processing of jobs, the data files that were mounted on the system, and other significant events. The operator's knowledge that the console log is reviewed deters information-security incidents in itself.

Measurement logs can record either all or part of the activity which takes place within a system. These logs can provide a complete audit trail of who accessed certain data or can record periodically the activity on certain files, should there be a need.

Management should receive records of all accesses to top-secret data and changes to the authorization tables (such as passwords and lock words) on a periodic basis. This information helps them monitor the activities of their function competently.

Violation logs report to management illegal attempts to access a terminal or data.

The secure system must be able to identify all attempted violations —- accidental or malicious. Any mismatch of user or terminal identification, password or lock word, or any unauthorized request for processing or data requires some reaction. At a minimum, the system should record the attempt in a log.[27]

Checklist 18
Auditability

☐ 1. Are adequate records kept of all attempts to access proprietary information?

☐ 2. Is a record kept of all authorized accesses that clearly identifies the data accessed, who accessed it, and when?

☐ 3. Is a periodic report of all authorized accesses to top-priority information or changes to the authorized access tables provided to management?

☐ 4. Is management provided with timely reports of unauthorized access attempts?

☐ 5. Does management use the provided reports?

☐ 6. Is the record-retention period adequate for these logs?

Cryptography

The military coded information to conceal its contents and protect communications long before the computer was ever invented.

---

[27] Op cit., Considerations of Physical Security, p. 20.

Traditional cryptography methods have been improved; and newer encryption techniques, certified by the National Bureau of Standards, have been developed for use in a data processing environment.

Cryptography can be applied to the transmission of data, including terminal communications and bulk transmission, and to the storage of data on files. It provides protection against wiretapping or a perpetrator's access to that data.

Cryptography should make the unauthorized use of data so inexpedient and costly that it would be uneconomical even to attempt access. Cryptographic techniques vary in complexity; but, in general, they provide an economical means of protecting highly proprietary information. Computer installations should make encryption available to their users, and users of the installations should take advantage of this security technique.

However, while cryptography does provide a relatively economical protection, there is a cost in terms of dollars and system resource. Encryption of too much data can result in a degradation of available system resource; therefore, care must be taken to ensure that files are not encrypted unnecessarily.

The auditor's review determines if key files are being encrypted and if the encryption methods are being employed in a conscientious manner. Poor practices can defeat the benefits to be gained from encryption. The success of encryption depends on how the "key" or security code necessary to decrypt the file is safeguarded.

Checklist 19
Encryption

☐ 1. Does the computer center provide tools for encryption of data in storage or during transmission?
☐ 2. Have the users requested encryption protection for key files?
☐ 3. Review encryption procedures.
☐ 4. Are encryption keys classified top-priority and protected as such?

Top-priority Information

Top-priority information should not be stored in data processing environment unless it can be afforded the same level of security and accountability there as it would have otherwise. Strict precautions should be taken to ensure that top-priority information is adequately protected. For example, the specific location of these files should be known at all times; they should be locked in an acceptable cabinet when they are not in use; a separate log should record their use, creation, or destruction, and a physical inventory should be taken frequently (perhaps weekly). Access to top-priority information must still be controlled by the top-priority document control center; however, it is necessary that some authority be delegated to the computer center. The additional controls required to protect top-priority information are outlined in the following checklist.

Checklist 20
Top-Priority Data

☐ 1. Does the DP function have a documented information-security plan specifying how it will protect top-priority data?

☐ 2. Has user management adequately identified the top-priority data to DP management?

☐ 3. Is access to all top-priority data authorized?

☐ 4. Is the location of top-priority data known at all times?

☐ 5. Are on-line media containing top-priority data taken off line immediately after use?

☐ 6. Are all top-priority media, tapes/disks, stored in a separately locked cabinet within the library or within the computer center?

☐ 7. Are these media inventoried weekly?

☐ 8. Do all bulk transmissions of top-priority data require the approval of the top-priority document control center?

☐ 9. Are all transmissions of top-priority data directed to the top-priority document control center at the receiving location?

☐ 10. Is the top-priority document control center involved in the remote computing of top-priority data?

☐ 11. Is all top-priority output distributed only by the top-priority document control center?

☐ 12. Does a complete record of all accesses to top-priority data in a DP environment exist? (Top-priority data should not be processed in a DP environment if this record does not exist.)

☐ 13. Are top-priority data encrypted for transmission and storage?

Summary

Data security is important and must be properly integrated into a company's total information-security program. Although much information is created in a computer center, total concentration on data security while ignoring other aspects of information security could be dangerous. The information stored and processed in a computer center is used elsewhere.

The amount of security which can be afforded should be assessed before putting sensitive information in a data processing environment. Sensitive information should not be put in a data processing environment until it can be given proper protection. This is obviously one way to eliminate data-security exposures.

Because of the dynamics of computer technology, a company's data-security technology must keep pace with computer technology. Data security should never be given a back seat.

Developing an Information-Security Audit Program

While the ideas and discussions presented in the preceding chapters are simple and require only a commonsense management approach, a company must positively determine that it has an effective information-security program; it cannot simply assume that it has. Such an assumption by either a company's internal audit staff or executive management could be disastrous in today's business environment.

The implementation of an effective information-security program requires developing an audit approach, writing a checklist, and educating the auditors. Only by developing a checklist tailored to meet the specific information-security needs of a company, designing an audit approach which will ensure that an information-security audit is carried out in the best possible manner, and giving the auditors the training they require will a complete and comprehensive information-security audit program result.

The preceding chapters have pointed up the areas of a business where information-security exposures may exist, and they have set forth the framework in which to conduct an information-security audit. The remainder of this chapter makes recommendations for developing an information-security audit program and suggests approaches to conducting an information-security audit.

Getting Management's Attention

As previously stated, executive management support is the most important ingredient of an effective information-security program. Without that, the benefits ensuing from information-security audits will be minimal. In developing an information-security audit program, determining the level of concern and support that can be expected from executive management is the first step. In organizations where the level of executive management concern and support is high, the audit organization will be well on its way to conducting effective audits of information security.

Effective audits are ones that truly accomplish the desired results. If an audit report points out significant problems and executive management does not take the required action, then the audit is not effective. The auditor's job is not finished when the report is written; it is finished when the program is solved. The implementation of an effective information-security program may take years because of the fact that it encompasses most, if not all, areas of the organization.

The audit staff must convince apathetic executive management of the need for an effective information-security program. A number of outside sources can bolster efforts in this direction.

Various U.S. governmental agencies, including the Department of Commerce and the Department of Defense, prepare publications that are extremely helpful. One, *The Cost of Crimes Against Business* offers a good overall perspective on the security issue. Another source, The Practising Law Institute, has a patents, copyrights, trademarks, and literary property handbook series (G-4-0009). Legal implications and court cases pertaining to information-security breaches are presented. Current literature and news items often demonstrate or reinforce the need for information security.

Executive management may not be aware of actual internal information-security incidents that have taken place within the organization; or they may have forgotten them — particularly in large organizations. Documenting or compiling a history of actual incidents within the organization is probably the most effective means to capture management's attention.

If the audit results point out that fundamental and recurring information-security deficiencies exist and management seems apathetic, it may be advisable (without the use of audit privilege) to demonstrate the need for information security by perpetrating an incident where highly proprietary information is obtained in an unauthorized and undetected manner. While such penetration attempts may be viewed as an extreme measure, they serve a useful and necessary purpose in some situations. They must, of course, be carried out in an intelligent and professional manner. Penetration attempts are discussed in more detail later in this chapter.

The audit report, obviously, is the tool most readily available to the auditor to present information-security exposure to management. The audit report formally expresses the auditor's concern. A properly written report elicits the needed response from management, whereas a poorly written one does just the opposite and can even destroy the auditor's creditability. The proper presentation of an information-security audit report is also discussed later in this chapter.

In summary, executive managers' support of information security can be bolstered by bringing to their attention:
• published statistics, legal implications, and court cases relating to information-security breaches
• a documentation of internal incidents

- the results of penetrations made without the use of audit privilege
- the results of the audit

Six Audit Approaches

The approaches to conducting an information-security audit will vary according to the organization's needs. Also, several of the following approaches may be combined in one audit:

- procedure review
- complete information-security audit
- selective information-security audits
- modular audits of information security
- audit penetrations
- complete security audit

Procedure Review

The purpose of reviewing corporate or organizational procedures is to determine if clear and precise statements defining the responsibilities and the requirements of the information-security program have been written and disseminated within the organization. The auditor using this approach should review the actual corporate guidelines, interview managers of the particular functions who are expected to comply with those guidelines, and combine the results in the audit assessment. The auditor must be careful in evaluating information obtained by interviewing management. Managers tend to criticize documents they must comply with. Generally, they will complain that the guidelines are not specific enough in telling how to accomplish the objectives.

Good information-security guidelines do not necessarily have to be specific at a detail level. They should clearly define the objectives but leave to operating management the best method of implementation for the environment. However, certain key areas, particularly those affecting multiple sites (top priority or bulk transmission), need specific and detailed procedures. A good information-security procedure clearly defines the purpose of what is to be accomplished, is comprehensive in coverage, and provides reasonable information security without significantly impacting the needs of the business.

Though a review of the organization's procedures for information security should be one of the initial audits, the auditor can conduct organization-wide procedures concurrently with audits of information security at a location. The results of location audits often support the need for improved procedures.

Complete Information-Security Audit

Conducting a complete review of all aspects of information security within a location at the same time is extremely beneficial for initially determining the state of the practice. Such a review concentrates on the functions where good information security should be implemented and covers all the areas outlined by the 20 checklists in this handbook. The results of these reviews from different locations will indicate to executive management the state of information security, organization-wide, and will identify problem areas (for example, data security) that require additional audit emphasis. Follow-up audits should concentrate on these problem areas.

Audit staffs not previously involved in information security should follow their audit of procedures with complete audits of information security at several locations. Complete information-security reviews accomplish four objectives. In addition to providing management with a knowledge of the state of the practice and identifying problem areas, they indicate to employees organization-wide that executive management is serious about maintaining information security. For audit teams not previously involved in information security, they provide an excellent source of on-the-job education prior to their concentrating on some of the more specialized audits.

Selective Information-Security Audits

This audit reviews the security of top-priority information as defined by location management or by the auditors with concurrence by location management. The auditors select one or several of the key information assets and evaluate how well it is protected in *all* areas where it is maintained. If the key information selected is not maintained in an area (for example, data processing), that area would not be subject to this type of review. In areas where the selected information is maintained, the scope of the review will be limited to the processing of the selected information. Audit findings not specifically related to the processing of the selected information will be incidental to the purpose of the review.

The complete information-security review concentrates on functions. This review concentrates on the most valuable information. The distribution of the information determines the scope of the audit. The auditors determine how the information is kept secure wherever it is disseminated; thus, the scope could be multilocational, multidivisional, or multinational.

This audit approach, concentrating on the most valuable resources, is highly effective in gaining management's attention. For example, an audit finding such as "The copy machines should be locked after hours" will cause less executive management concern than a finding such as "our after-hours tour disclosed that the complete new product design specifications were left on a desk top and there was an operational copier in an area where cleaning personnel were working unsupervised."

If, during a selective protection audit, the auditors feel that a significant exposure to loss of the selected information exists, they should attempt a penetration by making sure to follow the rules discussed later in this section.

Whether or not the approach is a selective information-security audit, the auditor should determine if management has effectively implemented the selective information identification and protection technique (as discussed in Chapters 3 and 4). The selective approach is the key to effective information security.

Modular Audits of Information Security

Either *complete* or *selective* audits of information security will identify areas where controls appear not to be well implemented. A modular audit of information security singles out an area of concern and spotlights it for executive management. Data security, being a more complex area, probably will require the special attention of a modular information-security audit focusing all the audit resources on one subject. Modular audits on one subject in multilocations and multidivisions will identify trends to executive management. For example, if the guidelines for data security are not clearly understood, they can cause an organization-wide problem. Modular audits identify these types of problems and are helpful in getting them solved.

The modular security audit can also provide more frequent audit coverage of information security at a location since fewer audit resources are called for in a smaller-scoped review. Frequent modular audits can serve to keep location management aware of the need for information security.

Audit Penetrations

The subject of audit attempts to penetrate the information-security system is controversial and may not have support in some organizations; however, this writer believes it is an effective and necessary tool if used judiciously. Its opponents argue that management implements controls when exposures are identified and that penetration attempts are unnecessary — even unprofessional. The argument carries weight if auditors continually try to "beat the system" to dramatize their concerns without good reason. However, audit penetrations are a valid approach to resolving significant concerns that have been previously brought to management's attention and remain unresolved.

An audit penetration dramatizes the need for resolution, but the auditor must not use audit privilege in accomplishing it. For a penetration to be successful, the auditor must demonstrate that the act could have been performed by another employee or, even better, by an outsider. He or she must also prove that audit privilege was not a factor in the penetration.

Another aspect to consider is: if the attempted penetration

is thwarted, it will probably reassure local management that its controls are adequate.

Executive management must know about and consent to the penetration attempt. Also, the actual attempt must be controlled to prevent putting the auditor in a position to compromise highly proprietary information without detection.

Carrying out a penetration can often be very simple. An example of a typical penetration would be accessing a terminal area in a highly sensitive area after hours, obtaining a password and system instruction manual that was not secure, and using the information to obtain access to highly proprietary information. This penetration, however, should not be attempted unless the insecure housekeeping practices had been pointed out to management previously and it had been determined in advance that the access would not be detected by a log.

In summary, a penetration attempt should only be carried out when:
1. an exposure to very sensitive information exists
2. the exposure is recurring and unresolved by management
3. the probability of success is almost certain
4. audit and executive management approval is obtained
5. audit privilege is not used
6. it can be demonstrated that any employee or nonemployee with access to the building could have done the same thing

Audit penetrations, while unorthodox, can be highly effective when performed for an explicit purpose in a well-controlled and professional manner. The auditor can easily gain executive management's attention on the subject of information security when he or she can present the design specifications of a new product obtained without the knowledge of functional management — especially if he or she can demonstrate that any subcontract cleaner could have done the same thing.

Complete Security Audit

Many of the information-security controls can be applied to other aspects of security. Information security can be covered as part of an overall security audit, but this approach is not recommended in organizations where information security is of paramount importance. The complete security audit, however, obtains the broadest coverage in a single audit.

Audit Checklist

The various checklists already presented form a sound base from which to develop an information-security checklist tailored to the needs of an individual organization. In developing the checklist, the auditors should solicit the cooperation, assistance, and concurrence of other corporate managers and their staffs in such departments as security, record management, data processing, law, personnel, and finance. Communication with these departments ensures that the resulting information-security reviews will concentrate on the right areas of the business. Communication helps in effectively assessing the information-security posture of the entire company and in reporting exposures to the appropriate management.

An effective information-security procedure must be tailor-made to suit the needs of the organization. Using a general checklist (such as presented in this handbook) without tailoring it to the organization's environment will result in important areas being overlooked.

The information-security checklist should also be referencing applicable company procedures and highlighting all the possible areas to be reviewed. The collective judgment of the internal auditor and the manager determines where to concentrate the review efforts. A 100-page, detailed checklist requiring the auditor to answer every question will not result in an effective information-security audit. The checklist for an effective information-security audit outlines the areas to be reviewed and the types of controls needed. It also gives the auditor and audit manager some leeway to exercise their judgment.

Audit Assistance

Knowledgeable employees from other functions can assist on a cooperative basis in conducting information-security reviews. For example, a knowledgeable employee from an information-systems function of another location or division or from the corporate staff could provide valuable technical expertise. Employees from security, information security, record management, data processing, legal, personnel, finance, and new product development all have valuable knowledge and experience to contribute.

Companies which have used co-ops to assist on internal audits have found the experience rewarding to both the internal audit staff and the function from which the employee was borrowed. When the internal audit staff can draw upon the knowledge of the co-op, it shortens the number of days expended and enables a more effective review of new areas such as data security. The co-op, in turn, gets an opportunity to get out into the field, learn audit techniques, and see what his or her peers are doing about information security. A co-op from division or corporate headquarters will experience some of the problems that location management is faced with and get a firsthand understanding of the environment. A co-op from another location or division will both acquire and impart knowledge regarding different and, perhaps, better methods of doing things.

The co-op should, of course, have a specific body of knowledge relevant to the particular audit. Also, regardless of the co-op's level within the company, the internal auditor is the audit leader.

He or she is the one who has been trained to conduct such reviews and report the results.

Minimally, communications with the corporate staffs in the noted functions can provide direction and answers to auditors conducting these reviews.

Conducting the Audit

An information-security audit requires the auditor to review the procedures of many functions. The number of functions encompassed and the degree of importance of information security to the company may require a change in the normal audit approach.

Preaudit Strategy

The internal auditor should spend one or two days reviewing the checklist, reading information-security audits conducted at other locations, talking to other auditors who have conducted information-security audits, and becoming familiar with the applicable material. The auditor then develops a general plan as to how the audit is to be conducted, based on his or her knowledge of the location to be audited. The plan should be discussed with the manager prior to starting the audit.

Audit Kick Off Meeting

The executive management at the location being audited and the manager of the security department should be present at the audit kick off meeting. The objectives of this meeting are to define the general scope of the audit and the approach to be used and to identify the most sensitive areas within that location as well as other areas of concern. The decisions reached pinpoint for the auditor the most important areas at that location and any other concerns location management may have.

Executive managers should notify their staffs that the audit is being conducted and request cooperation with the auditor. Eliminating as much red tape as possible helps the auditor in reviewing the many functions to be included in the audit.

The security department should be established as the auditor's primary interface. Because of the many functions to be reviewed, it would be impractical for the auditor to carry on discussions with all levels of management within each function being reviewed. The security department should act as communicant of the auditor's concerns. In this way, the concerns can be verified and, where possible, immediate corrective action taken.

Audit Technique

Whenever possible, the auditor should deal directly with the employee performing the duties being reviewed. However, to prevent the employee having apprehension about talking with the auditor, the first-line manager should introduce the auditor to the employee involved. The auditor should inform the first-line manager of security exposures as they are discovered. By dealing directly with the employees and keeping first-line management informed, the auditor can conduct the review faster, more effectively, and with a minimum of misunderstanding.

The auditor should inform the security department of concerns as they turn up rather than waiting until the end of the audit. The security department will then have opportunity to discuss the concerns and possible solutions with all levels of management within the function, take corrective action when possible, or discuss pertinent details with the auditor that may have been overlooked. By keeping the appropriate people informed about concerns as the audit progresses, a better working relationship will result; the final review meeting can be conducted with less discord; and, in general, the audit will be more effective.

After-Hours Tour

Toward the end of the audit, the auditor, accompanied by either the security department manager or an executive manager, should conduct an after-hours tour of the location being audited. This will reveal where the sensitive information resides within the building and what the after-hours procedures are to protect this information. During the after-hours tour, the auditor can assess whether perimeter and internal-security procedures are being followed and whether they are adequate.

The after-hours tour should include testing of perimeter-security controls (such as door locks and alarms); talking with guards at the control center; and, most especially, reviewing the after-hours security of sensitive areas within the building (such as new product development, trade-secret areas, finance, and the computer center).

Final Review Meeting

At the final meeting with the location's security department manager, the audit report is reviewed to ensure that there is agreement on the facts presented, to obtain the signature of the security manager, and to discuss the audit findings. Where the auditor was unable to make specific recommendations for some of the more difficult problems, possible solutions are discussed.

The security department manager does not have to agree with the opinions or recommendations expressed by the auditor. If there is disagreement the reasons should be stated in the security department manager's reply to the audit. The people reviewing the audit report will then have to decide whether the auditor's recommendations should be implemented.

Estimated Audit Days

Figure 4 presents an estimate of the number of man-days required to do an information-security audit. The total of 30 man-days is not based on anything so scientific as a time-and-motion study; it is based purely on the writer's judgment and is intended only as a guide for estimating how long it would take a single internal auditor or a group of internal auditors to conduct an information-security audit. The actual time will, of course, vary depending upon the particular circumstances of each company and of each location being audited within the company.

Figure 4
Estimated Audit Days

Subject		Audit Days
Preaudit strategy and initial audit meeting		2
Security organization		½
Perimeter and after-hours security		4
Entrances	½	
Employee identification	1	
Nonpermanent employee control	½	
Key control	½	
Guard duties	1	
After-hours tour	½	
Information service function		3
(Approximately 2 hours per function)		
Top-priority document control		2
New product security		4
(2 days per unannounced product)		
Trade secrets		4
(2 days per trade secret)		
Employee awareness		½
Destruction		½
Data security		6
Data processing organization	½	
Computer center access control	¼	
Data-access control	¾	
Tape and disk library	½	
Bulk transmission	¼	
Remote computing	3	
System design	½	
Top-priority information	¼	
Writing audit report and final meeting		3½
Total		30

The Information-Security Audit Report

The success of an information-security audit depends on the final audit report. This report expresses the auditor's concerns and will significantly influence the action taken to resolve them. Some organizations encounter difficulty in obtaining the necessary support for information security from executive management. The audit report is the auditor's primary vehicle for obtaining this support.

Intended Audience

The information-security audit report has two intended audiences: the executive management of the organization and the auditee.

The final report of a well-conducted audit should answer whether top-priority information is being afforded effective protection. This information should be provided to the highest executive officer of the organization. As stated before, an effective information-security program cannot exist without high-level support, and the auditor's job is not done until this support is obtained and significant corrective actions are taken.

The corporate and divisional staffs in functions such as security, data processing, and legal should also be kept informed about the status of information security.

Local management, as the auditee and second important audience, must understand the report to be able to take appropriate corrective action and respond with its plan. Response should be made within a specified period of time (30-40 days).

The auditor's written, detail report goes first to local security management. That management coordinates the replies of the various functions involved and responds to the highest executive manager on site. Copies of the audit reply go to the distribution list which includes executive management and appropriate corporate and divisional staffs. An executive summary of the detail report should state the audit results in brief but concise terms. Only the executive summary should be distributed to executive management, but the summary should note that the detail report is available on request.

The detail report and the executive summary ensure that local mangement is made aware of the specific problems it needs to address. At the same time, they serve as a status report and intended action plan for executive management. Executive management can either challenge the report and plan or follow up on them.

Format and Style

Generally, an executive summary should consist of one to three pages and should never exceed five. The information-security problem is only one of many concerns that management deals with on a day-to-day basis; there isn't time to read voluminous reports on any subject.

A recommended format for the executive summary is:

- purpose
- conclusion
- summary of findings
- environment
- scope of review

The purpose of the audit can be stated in a single sentence. The conclusion should be a stand-alone paragraph clearly stating whether significant concerns exist in the audited location and whether they require executive management's involvement. Deciding the significance of the findings is often the most difficult part of the audit. The concluding statement must be decisive, not a middle-of-the-road position. It is the auditor's responsibility to decide whether the information-security program is adequate or inadequate, and executive management expects that decision to be made.

An unsatisfactory conclusion requiring executive management's involvement must be based upon tangible audit findings. The auditor must be able to demonstrate that, as a result of the control problems noted, highly proprietary data is exposed to unauthorized access.

The audit report must also be well balanced and in perspective. If the management that has been audited has taken significant steps to improve information security or if there are valid mitigating circumstances, these facts should be clearly noted in the executive summary. In fact, where an effective information-security program exists the executive summary should be less than one page and should clearly state that as a conclusion. The comments section for audited management's response can include recommendations for enhancement or fine tuning.

Where an ineffective information-security program exists, there should be a summary of the significant findings that led to the unsatisfactory conclusion. The summary must discuss tangible and significant concerns worthy of executive management's attention. Problems of a lesser nature should be discussed in the detail section of the report.

The environment section discusses the characteristics of the audited location that relate to the type of information to be secured. It should speak to the purpose of the facility, the functions within it, and the characteristics (such as the number of people employed). It is also a good place to present mitigating circumstances that executive management should be made aware of (such as circumstances beyond the control of local management that require higher-level management intervention to resolve).

The scope of the audit should be discussed in the executive summary. Knowledge about the time and effort spent and the areas covered will assist executive management in evaluating the findings.

The detail report and the executive summary must obviously correspond to each other. However, since the detail report must clearly explain the problems, it is generally longer and more technical in nature. Each section of the audit report should be followed by the specific recommendations that the auditor thinks should be responded to. Numbering the recommendations will avoid misunderstandings as to what is expected in the reply. Audit recommendations must be reasonable. Unreasonable recommendations severely impact the ability to get the job done and may undermine the credibility of the information-security program.

Because the audit report includes both the executive summary and identification of information-security exposures, it is proprietary information and must be classified and protected accordingly. Minimally, an information-security audit report should be classified "priority."

Summary

An executive summary and a detail report are characteristic of an effective audit report. The style in which they are presented should be decisive, tangible, explicit, balanced, and reasonable.

7

Example of an
Information-Security Audit

If your company's internal audit staff has never conducted an information-security audit, the findings of the first audit will probably be astonishing to both the internal auditor and executive management; but the results to the company will be highly beneficial. This chapter presents what could be a typical audit report for a research and development location (fictitious) within a large corporation. It will give the reader an idea of the types of findings that might be discovered and, perhaps, reinforce the fact that there is a need to conduct an information-security audit.

Classified: Priority Information

Audit: Information Security
Location: R&D Division
To: Security Manager, R&D Location
c/c: Executive Management
Corporate and Division Staffs

EXECUTIVE SUMMARY

Purpose:

The purpose of our audit was to review the controls and procedures that exist to safeguard proprietary information in the research environment.

Conclusion:

The information-security program at the R & D Division is unacceptable, resulting in highly proprietary information (trade secrets, new product designs) being exposed to unauthorized and undetected loss. We acknowledge that, because of the flexibility required in a research environment, stringent security controls and procedures may hamper efficiency. However, as a result of our review, we highlight the following conditions in the summary of findings which, we feel, severely impact the overall security of the R & D Division and need immediate executive management attention.

Summary of Findings

• During our after-hours tour of the facility with senior site management, we obtained five prototypes of special part X and two bottles of a special chemical. They were unsecured in an area where subcontract cleaners were working unsupervised. All this material is top priority and subject to reverse engineering.
• Loss of top-priority documents from the control center could go undetected because of sloppy record keeping.
• New invention information that was not covered by patent protection was found unsecured.
• There was a lack of employee awareness of the need for information security and of their responsibilities.
• Access to highly proprietary data in the DP environment is not limited to a need to know. The information is exposed to unnecessary access.

Environment

We are particularly concerned with the security of this location because many of the ideas which are conceived here contribute substantially to the company's product line.

Scope of Review

Our review took 50 auditor-days and covered all 20 major areas of information security covered in the corporate procedures.

The details of this report are available upon request.

DETAIL REPORT

Security Organization

There is a lack of formal definition of the security responsibility of the facility-protection department (guard force) and of the site-security department. As a result, we find a duplication of effort in some areas. In other areas, as evidenced in this report, neither department has assumed the responsibility.

In addition, we note that security representatives have not been appointed within the functions at this location to work with the security department. The need for security representatives, at least within critical functions (such as new product development), is evident by the type of exposures discussed in the remainder of this report.

Recommendation: Clearly define information-security responsibilities and assign representatives.

Perimeter and After-Hours Security

External Doors

To facilitate the entrance of employees, all external doors remain unlocked from 7:30 until 9 a.m. to allow access to the building without the use of the employee's magnetic badge. We feel leaving the doors unlocked is unnecessary and creates a security exposure. In addition, the majority of research employees do not wear their badges. Thus, identification of a noncompany employee in the building would be difficult. We also point out that magnetic badges are issued to nonemployees (such as consultants and temporary help) and that adequate procedures are not in place to ensure their return.

Recommendation: Require the use of an employee's badge at all times. Require employees to wear their badges. Ensure adequate controls of nonemployee badges.

After-Hours Tour

Our after-hours tour of this location disclosed that a clean-desk policy is not in effect and that there is a lack of awareness or concern on the part of location employees to safeguard proprietary information. The condition of many of the offices in the building made it appear as if the employee were still working. Excessive accumulations of paper (i.e., computer printouts) were noted. Other than having information-security implications, this could be a potential fire hazard. We found information classified as priority exposed in many offices. Top-priority information was exposed in two offices.

During our review of the patent department, we found that, while this is a restricted access area, the subcontract cleaner signs out for the key at the guard control center and is allowed access to clean this area unsupervised. We also found that dockets are not locked up after hours and that, as a result, the cleaner had access to them. Some of the dockets discovered during our tour contained information on inventions for which a patent had not yet been filed.

Further investigation disclosed that this situation existed because patent department management assumed the cleaners were supervised by the guards; and the facilities protection department assumed the clean-desk policy was being observed and that all the classified information was locked up within the patent area. A similar situation existed in the new product function. This is discussed later in this report.

Recommendation: Management should review and strengthen after-hours security practices of all sensitive areas.

Guard Control Center/Tours

During our after-hours tour, we noted that the guard control center was manned by a college student who had been hired temporarily for the summer. We feel that the responsibilities associated with manning the control center which monitors after-hours security and emergency activity require the experience and dedication of a full-time employee.

Other college students are used to perform roving guard duty on site. Since it is necessary for the guards to access restricted areas to perform a tour, we question whether it is advisable to have temporary employees performing this function. We acknowledge that management elected to operate in this manner as a result of personnel constraints and vacation schedules.

Recommendation: Temporary employees should not perform guard tours.

Key Control

The facility protection department is not aware of the number of keys that have been issued for external or internal door locks. Their records indicate only the key number and the door for which it is issued. As a result, a ready reference to all keys and persons concerned is not available.

We acknowledge that, under present procedures, keys are issued to management only and that management is responsible for distribution. However, we do not feel that the present records and procedures provide effective control of the key network.

Also, we are concerned that more than 50 people, including all guards and maintenance personnel and executive management, possess a copy of the grand master key which allows access through all internal and external doors. We feel that this number is excessive and that only one or two people require a grand master key on a permanent basis. All other people with a legitimate temporary need should sign the key out from the guards' control desk.

Recommendation: Implement effective key controls.

Reproductions

This location has one central area where most of the bulk work is done, and many self-service reproduction machines are located throughout the building.

The self-service reproduction machines provide the opportunity for the unauthorized copying of top-priority or priority information. We feel that, at a minimum, these self-service reproduction machines should be rendered inoperable after hours, if they cannot be eliminated altogether and replaced by manned copy centers.

In the central reproduction area, all completed requests (including priority) are placed on an open shelf for customer pickup.

Classified scrap is being placed in cardboard boxes. Locked containers should be provided.

The central reproduction area is not housed within an island of security.

Recommendation: Management should implement corrective action to eliminate the four aforementioned deficiencies.

Top-Priority Document Control Center

Our review of top-priority document control procedures disclosed record-keeping problems resulting in weak accountability for top-priority documents.

Twelve boxes of top-priority documents waiting to be scrapped are being stored temporarily in a small room to which all the guards and maintenance personnel have a master key. The inventory records for top-priority documents show these documents already scrapped. As a result, the loss of one of these documents would not be detected. All top-priority documents should be stored in acceptable cabinets accessible only by the top-priority document control clerk and should not be removed from the inventory records until they are actually destroyed.

A sample of 40 top-priority documents disclosed the following discrepancies:

• Five documents which appeared on the inventory records to be signed out to individuals were still in the control center.

• Three documents marked as destroyed on the inventory records were still in the possession of the holder.

• Two documents in the holder's possession were not recorded at all on the inventory records.

The periodic inventories of top-priority documents are taken by the top-priority document control center clerk. To maintain a better separation of duties, the inventory of documents should be taken by an independent party.

No procedures exist for the destruction/retention of typewriter ribbons or magnetic cards or tapes used in the preparation of top-priority documents. Currently, the retention/destruction of these items is left to the discretion of the secretary.

Recommendation: Management should correct all the administrative deficiencies noted over the control of top-priority documents and conduct a thorough review.

New Product Security/Trade Secrets

While management has not developed a formal security plan for the new product they are working on, it identified that the uniqueness of the new product is dependent upon the processes used to develop part X and a special chemical, both of which have been identified as trade secrets. We were also advised that both part X and the special chemical are subject to reverse engineering.

As evidenced by our findings, management should conduct a comprehensive review of this new product, identify all the information associated with it, review the security protection afforded the information, and develop a detailed information-security program which should be approved by the security department.

After-Hours Security

During our after-hours tour of the facility with senior site management, we were able to obtain five prototypes of part X and two bottles of the special chemical. Senior site management immediately locked these items up in a vault. The items were found in unlocked areas within the restricted access area, and a subcontract cleaner was in the area unsupervised during our tour.

Laboratories

Within the island of security which houses the new product function, there are 15 individual laboratories that are all accessible with a common key. Approximately 75 employees have a copy of this key and can access all 15 laboratories. Management advised that only a few of these employees need access to more than one laboratory. We recommend that management consider equipping these laboratories with combination locks, that the combinations be unique for each laboratory, that they be changed periodically (monthly), and that they be disseminated only to those employees with a need to access that laboratory.

Prototype Accountability — Part X

A pilot line produces approximately 20 prototypes of part X a week. These are distributed to other functions at this location and to other company locations for testing purposes. While all of these prototypes are serialized and records are kept as they go through the various manufacturing processes, no reconciliation is made to ensure that all prototypes which start on the line are accounted for.

Also, while management advised that they notified the security departments at other locations as to the security precautions necessary to protect the prototypes, no procedures exist for notifying the receiving location that the prototypes have been sent, for obtaining receipt verification, or for controlling the final disposition of the prototypes after testing. Because of these deficiencies, we feel that the prototypes of part X are subject to undetected loss.

Documentation

As a result of our cursory review of unclassified information related to the new product, management classified two documents as top priority and five documents as priority to limit access to this documentation to only those with an authorized need to know. They also agreed to conduct a comprehensive review of the classification of all documentation associated with the new product.

Recommendation: Management should selectively identify all new product and trade-secret information and develop written security plans. Minimally, action should be taken on the concerns noted in this report.

Employees' Awareness

As previously mentioned, the majority of employees at this location do not wear badges as required, and much classified information is not locked up after hours. As a result, we feel that many of these employees are not aware of their responsibilities regarding information security. We also point out that, with the exception of an orientation for new personnel, there is no security education program for either employees or management at this location; the employees' news media are not utilized to reemphasize security; and, for the most part, security is not included as an item on employees' appraisals. The apparent reason for these deficiencies is that both the facility protection department and the security department thought these responsibilities belonged to the other department.

*Recommendation:*Immediate employees' awareness programs should be implemented.

Scrap

Priority scrap is picked up by the facilities protection department, packed in cardboard boxes, and transferred to the shipping and receiving dock where it is stored to await Wednesday pickup. Since truckers have frequent access to this area, we do not feel that adequate protection is given to these documents.

Recommendation: Adequately secure priority scrap.

Data Security

We have the following concerns regarding the security measures within the data processing function:

Organization

Data processing management has not established a security representative within the function. We feel the need for a DP security representative is critical in a research environment characterized by many small, scientific DP-installations in addition to the main administrative computer center. The security needs of the small installations are subject to dynamic change and must continually be reevaluated.

Recommendation: Assign a DP security representative.

Computer Center Access Control

Programmers are allowed unlimited access to the administrative computer center. Since they should require access only infrequently, we recommend that programming access to the computer room be controlled. Programmers should not be given magnetic badges allowing them unlimited access; they should be required to sign in and out when they do have need of access.

Also, five of the small computer installations are not housed within islands of security. While management advised that the information in these installations is not proprietary, we feel that, at a minimum, these installations should be locked after hours to protect the hardware and prevent unauthorized use of the equipment.

Recommendation: Implement effective access control of the computer installations.

Tape and Disk Library

• Classification: Approximately 60% of the 25,000 tapes in the library are not classified. Therefore, it is difficult to determine whether they should truly be unclassified or whether the classificaton process was overlooked. We recommend that computer center management survey the proprietors to determine if the tapes should be classified (top-priority, priority, or confidential) or unclassified. The tapes should then be labelled properly.

• Top-Priority: For vital records backup, some top-priority tapes are transferred on a weekly basis to an off-site storage facility. These top-priority tapes are packed in cardboard boxes which do not provide adequate protection. We recommend that suitable metal containers which can be locked be used.

We also note that the destruction of top-priority data is not being witnessed by two employees.

Recommendation: Correct the administrative deficiencies noted in the media library.

Bulk Transmission

No records are maintained to record the transmission or receipt of priority files. Such documentation should be maintained to provide an audit trail.

Recommendation: Maintain adequate records to record the bulk transmission and receipt of data.

Remote Computing

Our review of one terminal system containing top-priority and priority information with 1,500 users (both at this location and other company locations) disclosed the following concerns:

• Terminal security: Neither the terminals nor the terminal rooms on site are equipped with locks to prevent unauthorized use. Management should consider purchasing the lock features for the terminals or house the terminals in locked rooms.

• Sign-on codes: The administrator of the individual security codes for this system had not changed the security codes in over one year.

Since this system contains top-priority information, we feel the security codes should be changed on a more frequent basis (monthly).

• Data-access control: This terminal system allows access control down to the field level within a record. We do not feel the financial-planning application for the access-control routine is being administered properly. Four top-priority files exist for this application, and data-access control is administered at the file level rather than at the record level. This means that, if a user is authorized access to that file for his or her location's records, he or she has access to the same records for the ten other locations, even though he or she may not have a need to know. By administering access control within this application at the record level instead of at the file level, a user could be restricted to only that data for the location. Since these four files are classified top-priority, limiting access to the data on them to only those employees with a need to know is critical.

• Privileged sign-on codes: The privileged sign-on codes issued for this system allow complete access to all the data in the system, the establishment of new user's sign-on codes, and new privileged sign-on codes. At the time of our audit, management was unaware of how many people possessed a privileged sign-on code. Our review disclosed that at least 25 employees have this code. In our opinion, this seriously jeopardizes the security of all the information in this system including the top-priority financial files. These individuals run the spectrum from computer operators to the system programmers. Further discussion with management disclosed that only two of these individuals actually needed the privileged sign-on codes. Management took immediate corrective action and established strict approval procedures for the issuance of privileged sign-on codes.

The master-user listing containing all users' names and complete sign-on codes, including privileged sign-on codes, is not classified. In addition, it is kept in a regular filing cabinet. Since unauthorized access to this listing would allow a total compromise of the entire data base, it is our feeling that this listing should be classified top-priority and protected accordingly.

• Logs: The system provides the capability to report unauthorized attempts to access data. This capability is not being utilized.Management should provide this report to the users with top-priority data files at a minimum.

Recommendation: Implement controls to resolve the five remote-computing exposures identified.

System Design and Programming

The information systems development group at this location, comprising appoximately 200 people, is responsible for the development, installation, and maintenance of all research division applications.

Their development guideline does not require that security concerns in new applications be separately identified and reviewed during the development cycle. It is our opinion that security concerns should be explicitly stated in the design specifications of future applications, that one individual should be assigned the responsibility for security for each new application, and that the attainment of these security objectives should be reviewed during the various development phases.

Recommendation: Revise the management process for design to ensure that information security is explicitly documented in system documentation and effectively covered during the various phases.

Cryptography

The use of cryptography is nonexistent in this location. In our opinion, management should conduct a comprehensive review to determine whether cryptography should be used to store and transmit top-priority data.

Recommendation: Implement encryption capability for key data.

Weekend Coverage

Only one employee works in the computer center on weekends. That employee requires access to all top-priority data to perform his or her duties. Since there is no control to ensure that this employee does not misappropriate top-priority data, we recommend that management assign more than one employee and/or establish appropriate measures to resolve this separation-of-duty problem.

Recommendation: One employee should not be given complete access to sensitive data.

Accepting the Challenge

Much of the literature today regarding industrial security or data security deals with security related to the prevention of fraud or embezzlement, and most security incidents reported involve the misappropriation of company funds. This is not surprising because fraud and embezzlement generally take place over a prolonged period of time and require the alteration of information. Information needs to be stolen only once, and the act does not require alteration or even the removal of the document the information is recorded on.

The fact that many incidents of information-security breaches have not been reported does not mean that they are not occurring. It may mean that the information and data-security precautions used by industry today are not even effective for detection, let alone prevention. It stands to reason that perpetrators are going to concentrate on the area of a business where the rewards are high and the risks are low. Using this criterion, a company's sensitive information is much more vulnerable to loss than any other asset. Thus, the future of many companies may depend upon the effectiveness of their information-security programs.

If a business is going to survive in today's environment, executive management must ensure that an effective information-security program is in existence company-wide. Because of the negative nature of information security and the fact that new media for the creation and transmission of information are continually being invented, there must be a continued vigilance and reevaluation of a company's information-security program. A company's information-security technology must not fall behind information processing technology.

An information-security audit serves several purposes besides pointing out information-security exposures. Through the audit reports, management is able to assess whether an effective information-security program is in place company-wide and whether the company's information-security technology is keeping pace. The information-security audit will also serve as a reminder to location management and employees that corporate management is concerned about information security. It lets them know that the company is committed and that information-security exposures will not be tolerated. Last, the information-security audit acts as a deterrent in itself. People are apt to do a better job of information security when they know that someone will review their work and report the results to higher management.

The internal audit profession must accept the challenge and develop an effective information-security audit program to assist management in assessing the information-security posture of its company. It is hoped that the framework presented here will be of assistance.

Internal auditors, armed with a checklist tailor-made to the needs of their company and sufficient background knowledge in data security, will immediately detect significant information-security exposures within any company.

It takes years to develop an effective information-security program; now is the time to get started.

BIBLIOGRAPHY

Books

Black, Henry C. *Black's Law Dictionary*. St. Paul, Minnesota: West Publishing Company, 1951.

Canadian Institute of Chartered Accountants. *Computer Control Guidelines*. Toronto: The Canadian Institute of Chartered Accountants, 1973.

Canadian Institute of Chartered Accountants. *Computer Audit Guidelines*. Toronto: The Canadian Institute of Chartered Accountants, 1975.

Healy, Richard J. *Design for Security*. New York: John Wiley and Sons., Inc., 1968.

Mair, William; Wood, Donald; and Davis, Keagle. *Computer Control and Audit*. 2nd ed. revised. Altamonte Springs, Florida: The Institute of Internal Auditors, Inc., 1978.

Jancura, Elise G., and Berger, Arnold H., ed. *Computers: Auditing and Control*. Philadelphia: Auerback Publishers, Inc., 1973.

Jaspan, Norman. *Mind Your Own Business*. Englewood Cliffs, New Jersey: Prentice-Hall, 1974.

Katzan, Harry, Jr. *Computer Data Security*. New York: Van Nostrand Reinhold Company, 1973.

Martin, James. *Security, Accuracy, and Privacy in Computer Systems*. Englewood Cliffs, New Jersey: Prentice-Hall, 1973.

Newman, Oscar. *Design Guidelines for Creating Defensible Space*. U.S. Department of Justice, U.S. Government Printing Office, 1976.

Menboisse, Raymond M. *Industrial Security for Strikes, Riots and Disasters*. Springfield, Illinois: Charles C. Thomas Publishers, 1968.

Practising Law Institute. *Protecting and Profiting from Trade Secrets*. Course Handbook Series Number 83. New York: Practising Law Institute, 1977.

Prentice-Hall Encyclopedic Dictionary of Business Law (The). Englewood Cliffs, New Jersey: Prentice-Hall, 1961.

Ursic, Henry S., and Pagano, Leroy E. *Security Management Systems*. Bannerstone House, 1974.

Van Tassel, Dennis. *Computer Security Management*. Englewood Cliffs, New Jersey: Prentice-Hall, 1972.

Walsh, Timothy J., and Healy, Richard J. *Protecting Your Business Against Espionage*. New York: American Management Association, 1973.

Periodicals

Adelson, Alan M. "Computer Bandits." *True*, (February 1969): 50.

Allen, Brandt R. "Computer Security." *Data Management* (January 1972): 18-24.

Astor, Saul D. "The New Look in Corporate Security." *Business Management* (March 1969): 33.

"Computers and Auditing." *Datamation* (July 15, 1970): 108-113.

"Computer Security: The Imperative Nuisance." *Infosystems* (February 1974): 24-28.

Freed, Roy N. "Computer Fraud: A Management Trap." *Business Horizons* (June 1969): 29-30.

"My People Stealing? You Gotta Be Kidding!" *Industry Week* (March 26, 1973): 44.

Reber, Jan R. "The Essence of Industrial Espionage." *Asset Protection Journal*, Vol. I, No. 1 (Spring 1975).

Van Tassel, Dennis. "Information Security in a Computer Environment." *Computers and Automation* (July 1969): 24.

Newspapers

Allen, Henry. "Computer Crime." *The Record* (Bergen County, New Jersey). March 5, 1973.

Association and government publications

American Management Association. *Crimes Against Business Council.* American Management Association, December 1977.

Garrison, W.A., et al. *Privacy and Security in Data Banks.* Springfield, Virginia: National Technical Information Service, U.S. Department of Commerce, 1970.

IBM Corporation. *The Considerations of Data Security in a Computer Environment* (Form G520-2619-0). White Plains, New York: IBM Corporation, 1970.

IBM Corporation. *The Considerations of Physical Security in a Computer Environment* (Form G520-2700-0). White Plains, New York: IBM Corporation, 1972.

IBM Corporation. *Forty-Two Suggestions for Improving Data-Processing Operations* (Form G520-2797-0). White Plains, New York: IBM Corporation, 1973.

Martin Marietta Aerospace. "A Contractor's Self-Inspection Program." Richmond, Virginia: Martin Marietta Aerospace, 1973.

National Bureau of Standards. *Audit and Evaluation of Computer Security.* National Bureau of Standards Publication 500-19. Washington, D.C.: U.S. Government Printing Office.

National Bureau of Standards. *Guidelines for Automated Data Processing Physical Security and Risk Management.* Federal Information Processing Standard Publication No. 31. Washington, D.C.: U.S. Government Printing Office, 1974.

Systems Auditability and Control (3 vols.). Altamonte Springs, Florida: The Institute of Internal Auditors, Inc., 1977.

U.S. Department of Defense. *Industrial Security Manual For Safeguarding Classified Information.* Alexandria, Virginia: Defense Supply Agency, 1970.

U.S. Department of Defense. *Industrial Security Regulation.* Alexandria, Virginia: Defense Supply Agency, 1970.